Palgrave Studies in Risk, Crime and Society

Series Editors

Kieran McCartan
Dept of Criminology, University of the West of England, Bristol, United Kingdom

Philip N. S. Rumney
University of the West of England
Bristol, United Kingdom

Nicholas Ryder
University of the West of England
Bristol, United Kingdom

Risk is a major contemporary issue which has widespread implications for theory, policy, governance, public protection, professional practice and societal understandings of crime and criminal justice. The potential harm associated with risk can lead to uncertainty, fear and conflict as well as disproportionate, ineffective and ill-judged state responses to perceived risk and risky groups. Risk, Crime and Society is a series featuring monographs and edited collections which examine the notion of risk, the risky behaviour of individuals and groups, as well as state responses to risk and its consequences in contemporary society. The series will include critical examinations of the notion of risk and the problematic nature of state responses to perceived risk. While Risk, Crime and Society will consider the problems associated with 'mainstream' risky groups including sex offenders, terrorists and white collar criminals, it welcomes scholarly analysis which broadens our understanding of how risk is defined, interpreted and managed. Risk, Crime and Society examines risk in contemporary society through the multidisciplinary perspectives of law, criminology and socio-legal studies and will feature work that is theoretical as well as empirical in nature.

More information about this series at
http://www.springer.com/series/14593

Abdullahi Usman Bello

Improving Anti-Money Laundering Compliance

Self-Protecting Theory and Money Laundering Reporting Officers

palgrave
macmillan

Abdullahi Usman Bello
Forensic Accounting and Financial Investigation
Economic and Financial Crimes Commission
Abuja, Nigeria

Palgrave Studies in Risk, Crime and Society
ISBN 978-3-319-43263-2   ISBN 978-3-319-43264-9 (eBook)
DOI 10.1007/978-3-319-43264-9

Library of Congress Control Number: 2016948409

Printed on acid-free paper

This Palgrave Macmillan imprint is published by Springer Nature
The registered company is Springer International Publishing AG
The registered company address is: Gewerbestrasse 11, 6330 Cham, Switzerland

To my wife, Hadiza Abdullahi, the mother of my two lovely children; Muhammad and Usman

Foreword

As these words are crafted, money laundering is centre stage both in connection with the leaked Panama papers and the perceived risks posed by offshore finance centres (OFCs) and with its link to corruption. Public disquiet over foreign criminals using OFCs as a means of 'laundering' their criminal assets through the London property market[1] appears to be prompting more overt action on the part of the UK Government with a series of recent announcements: requiring disclosure of owners of all overseas companies purchasing property in the United Kingdom (UK); a new corporate money laundering offence that would hold employers responsible for failing to prevent money laundering by their employees;[2] and plans for introducing the offence of 'illicit' enrichment for UK public servants.[3]

---

[1] Damien Gayle "Foreign criminals use London housing market to launder billions of pounds" The Guardian, 25th July, 2015. Available at: http://www.theguardian.com/uk-news/2015/jul/25/london-housing-market-launder-offshore-tax-havens.

[2] Patrick Wintour and Heather Stewart, The Guardian 12th May, 2016 "David Cameron to introduce new corporate money-laundering offence". Available at: http://www.theguardian.com/politics/2016/may/11/david-cameron-corporate-money-laundering-offence-anti-corruption-summit.

[3] BBC News "Money laundering: new law planned to target corrupt officials" 21st April, 2016. Available at: http://www.bbc.co.uk/news/uk-36098769.

If these proposals find their way onto the statute books, there will be yet more rules and regulations with which companies and institutions find themselves legally bound to comply. Of course public intervention within otherwise 'free markets' is predicated on the desire to correct some imperfection and indeed must be both justified and proportionate. This is especially the case when state intervention places burdens upon or intrudes into the lives of its citizens. Intervention in the financial market is more frequently justified because in its absence, the rest of the economy would fail to function. Writing almost thirty years ago, Lomax (1987) cited in Franks *et al.* (1998, p. 1548) makes a most salient observation *"the only major threat to the future health of the financial services industry is that of excessive or inappropriate legislation"*. For regulation is not cost neutral. Indeed in the UK each new law must be accompanied by a regulatory impact assessment (RIAs), a 'soft' cost-benefit assessment. 'Soft' because very often costs are only partially identified whilst claimed benefits are unquantifiable, presented in narrative terms. Thus, Harvey (2004) reviewed the RIAs for UK Money Laundering Regulations in 1993 and 2001 and demonstrated costs to be significantly understated and benefits unquantified merely promising sweeping protections for society from the global threat to the integrity of the financial system. Whilst no one would condone the activities of organised criminal gangs or of terrorists, they are very different both in objective and modus operandi but are within political discourse co-joined in creating the 'threat' giving absolute justification for the imposition of an extensive anti-money laundering (AML) regulatory framework.

Such burdens are not inconsequential. Harvey (2008) noted that the machinery of AML compliance had become self-generating with increasing cost implications. Those charged with their compliance within institutions can find themselves personally liable for failures within their organisation or by any of their employees to spot and report money laundering. Her respondents draw attention to their difficulties in coping and refer to a culture that is fear driven and risk avoiding. Those bearers of the poisoned chalice of AML compliance (Harvey, 2004) negotiate a tricky line between ensuring that they keep their employing firm on the right side of the law whilst ensuring that they do not overly inhibit the activity of those employed by the same company to seek out and exploit profitable business opportunities. After all, 'risk taking' is the pursuit of profitable opportunity whereby the risk being taken is assessed, measured and managed.

Concerns about costs arising from and associated with what became termed the 'rules-based' approach, an approach that was proving overly prescriptive and burdensome, resulted in banks lobbying hard for a change in which they both managed to bend the ear of the regulator[4] and were consulted on implementation of the revised 'risk-based' approach to AML compliance. Risk and the appropriate way in which it is handled has its roots in the insurance industry, where it was a relatively straightforward affair to assess the probability of a set possible incidents or events that have occurred within a defined time span to a particular subject. Then calculate the loss (for it is usually a one-sided affair) arising from its occurrence. In simple terms, risk = probability × impact. This quantitative assessment to risk was long ago adopted by the Bank for International Settlements and promulgated through its various Basel Accords for the measurement and management of risk within the global banking sector. As the main complaint with the cost of compliance with the original rule-based approach to AML compliance emanated from the banking sector, it was understandable that they would have been more receptive to a 'risk-based approach' (RBA) as this was familiar language.

The banks formed part of a group asked to develop guidance in relation to the RBA to foster a common understanding of what the term actually meant. Although the best this group could offer was that it "*. . . encompasses recognising the existence of the risk(s), undertaking an assessment of the risk(s) and developing strategies to manage and mitigate the identified risks*" (FATF, 2007[5] p. 2). This inability to capture what is meant by 'risk' within the arena of AML remains outstanding. Guidance

[4] See Financial Services Authority (FSA) "DP22: Reducing money laundering risk: know your customer and AML monitoring".

[5] FATF (2007), 'Guidance on the Risk-Based Approach to combating money laundering and terrorist financing' FATF/OECD, Paris.

notes on the RBA set out in the FATF 2013[6] (p. 4) methodology state that *"Once ML/TF risks are properly understood, country authorities may apply AML/CFT measures in a way that ensures they are commensurate with those risks—i.e., the risk-based approach (RBA)"*. Although there was no attempt to inform supervisors how they should set about assessing risk that being set out in the nine sectoral RBA guidance papers. The guidance for the banking sector,[7] however, lacks specificity making application of the approach even more challenging, adding a new dimension of 'interpretation risk' when the assessment of the bank fails to accord with that of the regulator (see also Demetis & Angell, 2007).

In a perfect world, banks should be able to objectively assess the probability that for the total number of transactions passing across their books 'x%' will likely be associated with criminal activity. Of course in and of themselves these will not necessarily be loss making, so will not be observable from any historic loss database, and so indicators and red flags have to be built up in more interpretative ways, hence the criticism that banks can only truly observe what is unusual (Favarel-Garrigues *et al.* 2008). Unfortunately, unlike 'risk taking', 'being at risk' lacks any objective rod of measurement. What is evident here is that despite application of common vocabulary, the interpretation of 'risk' within AML is fundamentally different[8].

It is this fundamental difference that Abdullahi Bello carefully lays out before us in this book. He is, of course, not the first to centre a PhD study on compliance officers, Antoinette Verhage conducted hers with Belgian compliance officials noting (2011, p. viii) that *'once they are*

[6] FATF (2013) Methodology For Assessing Technical Compliance With The FATF Recommendations And The Effectiveness of AML/CFT Systems, FATF/OECD, Paris, February.

[7] FATF (2014) 'Guidance For A Risk-Based Approach; The Banking Sector', FATF/OECD, Paris, October.

[8] For an elaboration of the general discussion about proportionality and the risk-based approach, see Van Duyne, Harvey and Gelemerova (forthcoming) 'The Monty Python Flying Circus of Money Laundering and the Question of Proportionality' Chapter in ' Illegal Entrepreneurship, 'Organised Crime' and Social Control: Essays in Honour of Professor Dick Hobbs' (ed) G. Antonopolous Springer, Studies in Organised Crime.

found, they are very interesting and intriguing conversation partners'. Research in this field is not to be undertaken lightly; compliance professionals are often reluctant to talk publically, being anxious not to express views that differ from those of their employers. So it is less usual for empirical work to focus on the personal challenges faced by this group of people. By employing a grounded theory methodology, Bello was able to hear first-hand about their concerns. Data collection was carried out just by listening, no recording or note taking to disturb the conversation flow with his respondents feeling able to talk more freely.

Through this approach he has been able to uncover the very personal narrative of their daily lives and work pressures—the criticisms of compliance officers as being seen as cost centres and profit inhibiting, squeezed between two masters—their employer on the one hand and the regulator on the other. They feel underappreciated, the object of opprobrium for their trading-based colleagues. He further clearly demonstrates how the move from a rules based to a risk-based approach far from improving matters has actually increased levels of uncertainty. This leads him to derive what he refers to as 'self-protecting theory'. This states that the more there is unfair pressures on compliance officers, the more they protect themselves rather than assist in regulation. However, rather than leaving things at this juncture he goes on to carefully construct an alternative approach to compliance that gives greater involvement to money laundering reporting officers as co-constructors of an AML framework in which they have control of their decision making.

This book makes an excellent contribution to literature on AML compliance, and as we enter the Fourth Round of FATF Mutual Evaluation, I recommend it as essential reading to policy makers.

Newcastle Business School,
Northumbria University

Professor Jackie Harvey

References

Demetis, D., & Angell, I. (2007). The risk-based approach to AML: Representation, paradox, and the 3rd directive. *Journal of Money Laundering Control, 10*(4), 412–428.

Favarel-Garrigues, G., Godefroy, T., & Lascoumes, P. (2008). Sentinels in the banking industry: Private actors and the fight against money laundering in France. *British Journal of Criminology, 48*(1), 1–19.

Franks, J., Schaefer, S., & Staunton, M. (1998). The direct and compliance costs of financial regulation. *Journal of Banking & Finance, 21*, 1547–1572.

FATF (2007). *Guidance on the risk-based approach to combating money laundering and terrorist financing*. Paris: FATF/OECD.

FATF (2013). *Methodology for assessing technical compliance with the FATF recommendations and the effectiveness of AML/CFT systems*, Paris: FATF/OECD.

FATF (2014). *Guidance for a risk-based approach; The banking Sector*. Paris: FATF/OECD.

Harvey, J. (2004). Compliance and reporting issues arising for financial institutions from money laundering regulations: A preliminary cost benefit study. *Journal of Money Laundering Control, 7*(4), 333–346.

Harvey, J. (2008). Just how effective is money laundering legislation? *The Security Journal, 21*, 189–211.

Lomax, D. (1987). *Financial markets after the financial services act*, London: Butterworths.

Verhage, A. (2011). *The anti money laundering complex and the compliance industry*. London: Routledge Studies in Crime and Economics Edited by Peter Reuter and Ernesto Savona.

Acknowledgements

I wish to start by thanking Allah, the most gracious and the most merciful, for his blessings and my parents Usman Bello Akko and Fatima Muhammad for their love and prayers.

I also acknowledge the support of Professor Jackie Harvey, Abubakar Usman Bello and Nuhu Bello Akko among others.

Contents

List of Figures

List of Tables

1

Introduction

There has been a lot of discussion about the level of effectiveness of anti-money laundering (AML) within the United Kingdom (UK) and even globally. Some have attributed the problem with AML to weak regulatory and compliance framework, others lay the blame on the regulated sector for not doing enough to prevent money laundering, while some have attributed the problem to the cost of compliance imposed by the regulators. This book looks at the problem of AML from the perspective of one of the most important stakeholders, the money laundering reporting officers (MLROs), because their voice is often not heard in the debate despite the critical role they play in AML.

Consequently, the chapter introduces the problem with AML from the perspective of MLROs. The aims and objectives of the book, the justification for the writing of the book and a brief discussion on the philosophy and methodology adopted for the research that underpinned the book are also included in the chapter.

A.U. Bello, *Improving Anti-Money Laundering Compliance*,
Palgrave Studies in Risk, Crime and Society,
DOI 10.1007/978-3-319-43264-9_1

Introduction

Money laundering is a global phenomenon that has been around for ages (Unger 2013a). In its basic form, it is the process of concealing of the source of illicit money. The problem with money laundering is that it encourages criminal activities, allow money launderers to benefit from the proceeds of their criminal activities and threatens the soundness of the financial system (Schott 2006).

As a result of these negative effects, the international community has introduced various initiatives to tackle the problem caused by money laundering. The main organisation that deals with the problem globally is the Financial Action Task Force (FATF), an institution formed by the Group of Seven most industrialised nations initially to deal with drug-related money laundering offences and later terrorist financing and other serious offences. The organisation developed 40 Recommendations in 1989 as a comprehensive measure to preventing money laundering. The recommendations were subjected to various amendments before the organisation finally adopted the Recommendations in 2012 for the prevention of money laundering, counter-terrorist financing and proliferation of weapons of mass destruction.

The United Nations (UN) was, however, the first to introduce a global measure to tackle the problem with the introduction of the UN Convention against Illicit Traffic in Narcotic Drugs and Psychotropic Substances in 1988. Later, the UN introduced other conventions, such as United Nations (2000) on Transnational Organized Crime and United Nations (2004) on Corruption, to widen the scope of predicate offences and adapt to changing money laundering schemes. Other institutions that are at the forefront of the fight against money laundering include the World Bank, IMF, Egmont Group and Wolfsberg Group.

The European Union (EU) is also active in combating money laundering. Countries in the EU are obliged to follow various Directives on money laundering that were passed mainly to implement the recommendations of the FATF. The first Directive was passed to give effect to the first forty Recommendations of the FATF, and when the recommendations were amended in 1996, a second Directive was issued. There is also the third

Directive that is more comprehensive, which broadened the scope of predicate offences, included other organisations as regulated entities and introduced a risk-based approach to AML. The Directive that is now in force is the fourth EU Directive, which was issued in 2015 to further address the threat of money laundering. Furthermore, member countries are required to comply with the Directive by June 2017 (European Union 2015).

The UK, being one of the major countries in the EU and a strong member of the FATF, is one of the most active countries in implementing various AML Directives and FATF recommendations (de Koker 2009), mainly through money laundering regulations (MLR). The first MLR was issued in 1993 to implement the first Directive, the second in 2003 to implement the second Directive and finally the MLR in force is the 2007 MLR regulation, which is essentially a regulation that gives effect to the third EU Directive (van den Broek 2011).

Several acts were enacted to support the fight against money laundering. These include the Proceed of Crime Act 2002 (PoCA 2002), which is the foremost legislation for dealing with money laundering. Before 2002 there were Drug Trafficking Act 1994 (DTA 1994), the Criminal Justice Act 1998 (CJA 1988) and the Terrorism Act 2000 (TA 2000) that were also related to the fight against money laundering. Several organisations were also created to enforce the provisions of the law. Some of the organisations include the Serious Organised Crime Agencies (SOCA) and the Financial Service Authority (FSA), which, though not mainly created for AML, had powers to implement AML regulations. These two organisations were replaced by the National Crimes Agency (NCA) and the Financial Conduct Authority (FCA), respectively, but they retain the same powers and responsibilities to prevent money laundering. The two agencies were created by the Crime and Courts Act 2013 and Financial Services Act 2012, respectively.

One industry that was subject to intense regulation regarding AML was the banking industry because of the belief that the majority of money laundering activities were conducted through the industry (Takats 2011). Banks were unwillingly recruited to support the fight against money laundering through requirements for them to implement systems and controls to deter the use of their system for the conduct of money laundering. Several other requirements were placed on the banks, but perhaps the most important requirement now is to appoint an MLRO to coordinate AML activities and liaise with regulators. The main duties of an MLRO are to identify and report suspicious money laundering activities within the bank to the regulators and to ensure that banks are complying with other MLRs.

The Purpose of the Book

The purpose of the book is, therefore, to provide an understanding of this regulatory environment, identify the problems affecting it and suggest solutions. To achieve this broad objective, it was decided that the best way is through understanding the concerns and behaviours of MLROs and discovering a grounded theory that would explain these concerns.

Justification of the Book

There are a lot of books and articles on money laundering, but most of the writings are conceptual; reviews and opinions and the empirical research in the field are mostly descriptive rather than theoretical (Demetis 2010). There is, however, research that deals with the regulatory issues, but most are looking at the effectiveness of the regulation from the perspective and based on the objectives of regulators. Examples of such studies are Takats (2011), Masciandaro (1999) and Araujo (2008). Other books in the area are focused on the effect and the typology of money laundering. The author, therefore, decided to write a theoretical book in order to contribute to knowledge in AML since according to Demetis (2010 p. 36), *"while these typological examinations remain useful for practitioners, academic research ought to be grounded on a theoretical level and assist in drawing the implication to practice".*

MLROs were eventually selected as participants for the research underpinning the book because they are at the heart of AML regulation given the responsibilities placed on them by law and the importance of their duties to preventing money laundering. Besides, there is surprisingly limited research on the role of MLROs despite their critical role in compliance. The two studies in the UK focusing on MLRO identified in the literature (Bosworth-Davies 1998; Webb 2004) are descriptive and dated.

This book is, therefore, an attempt to look at the problem of AML regulation from the perspective of MLROs and to discover a theory that would contribute to AML field that lacks a theoretical foundation.

The Aims and Objectives of the Book

Consequently, the main aim of the book is to explore the main concerns of MLROs in the UK banking industry in relation to the anti-money laundering legislative framework and to present a theoretical explanation of these concerns.

Specifically, the objectives are as follows:

- Provide an understanding of the AML environment from the perspective of MLROs.
- Discover concepts from their perspective that will explain their concerns and the ways of resolving them.
- Identify the main concern of MLROs and the core category that resolves it.
- Discover a theory that would explain how MLROs are resolving their main concern.
- Discover a framework that will explain the environment in which they operate.
- From the framework, suggest an effective and efficient approach to AML compliance.

To achieve these aims and objectives, the book seeks to find answers to two questions:

- What is the main concern of MLROs?
- How are they resolving their main concern?

These questions are based on the classical grounded theory approach for conducting research in which a researcher is advised to enter the field with as little preconception as possible and with no defined research problem or research question (Glaser 1998). As data are collected and analysed, the real research problems and research questions will evolve.

The answer to the first question denotes the problem facing MLROs and the answer to the second question becomes the core category that resolves the problem.

The main concern of MLROs from the research was found to be *unfair pressure* mainly from regulators, and the strategy for resolving this problem was through *protecting* themselves from the unfair pressure. Below is a summary of how the problem and the question emerged from the data.

Emerging Theory

The problem or the main concern that emerged was *unfair pressure*. *Unfair pressure* is a high-level concept formed from a combination of two concepts called *unfair* and *pressure*, which together conceptualised the main concern of MLROs. *Unfair pressure* comprises two concerns: regulatory concern and organisational concern. Under the regulatory concern are *defective regulations*, which represent regulations that MLROs consider faulty and ineffective; *shifting expectation*, which represents the continual changes in regulations and regulatory expectations and *damage to reputation* resulting from fear of prosecution, fine and penalties and naming and shaming strategy of the regulators. The final concern under this category is *naive regulators* that represent the lack of understanding of the banking environment and lack of skill and experience of some staff of regulatory institutions.

On organisational concern, this mainly relates to the concern of MLROs over *under resources* and *marginal management*. *Under resources* represents a situation where MLROs lack the time, human and financial resources to discharge their responsibilities while *marginal management* is a concept that represents the difficulties that MLROs face in managing employees that are outside their control. *Marginal management* is peculiar to MLROs and others in a similar situation where they have to deal with several other units that may not share in their objectives of preventing money laundering.

The answer to the second question dealing with how MLRO are resolving their main concern was found out to be *protecting*, a category that conceptualises the various strategies adopted by MLROs to deal with the *unfair pressure* exerted on them by regulators and banks. Two main protecting strategies are used to deal with the unfair pressure; the first is *discharging* and the second *communicating*. *Discharging* represents a situation where MLROs are doing just enough to satisfy the requirement of law, but not necessarily to prevent money laundering. It has five properties, namely *assessing*, *reporting*, *learning*, *automating* and *complaining*. *Discharging* is mainly used to deal with regulatory concerns, whereas *communicating* represent the strategy of MLROs for dealing with organisational concerns, and it has four properties namely *dialogue*, *threat*, *justifying* and *complaining*.

However, the *protecting* behaviour is moderated by another concept called *aligning*. An MLRO adopts discharging or *communicating* strategy based on his allegiance. MLROs that are *aligning* with banks and are under unfair *pressure* from regulators are *discharging* while MLROs that are *aligning* with regulators and are under *unfair pressure* from their banks are *communicating*. *Aligning* has two properties, that is, *interest* and *belief*. *Interest* is mainly in the form of *reward* and *punishment* while *belief* has *culture, ethics* and *conviction* as its three properties.

MLROs in the UK banking industry are constantly trying to balance conflicting pressure from the regulators on the one hand and banks on the other by using the *protecting* strategy. However, it was discovered that their main strategy is to deal with regulatory concerns mainly through *discharging* their responsibilities to protect themselves rather than *complying* with regulation to prevent money laundering. There are, however, instances where they are *communicating* to protect themselves against banks rather than *cooperating* to protect the interest of banks.

Based on these strategies and in line with the theoretical coding process in the classical grounded theory approach, the author used the paired opposite and degree theoretical codes to discover the *self-protecting* theory. The *self-protecting* theory, in essence, states that the more *unfair pressure* in exerted on MLROs the more they protect themselves.

Following from this theory, a framework was discovered to explain the various strategic options available to an MLRO depending on the nature of the *unfair pressure*. If the *unfair pressure* is coming from regulators and an MLRO is aligning with a bank, the strategy is *discharging*. If, however, the *unfair pressure* is coming from the bank and the MLRO is aligning with the regulators, the strategy is *communicating*. Similarly, when an MLRO is faced with fair pressure mainly from regulators and is aligned with the regulators, then the strategy is *complying*. If, however, the MLRO is aligned with the bank and there is fair pressure mainly from the bank, then the strategy is *cooperating*. This framework is important because it explains the possible behaviour of an MLRO when faced with different options. When the behaviours of individual MLROs are aggregate in an industry like the banking industry, for example, the predominant strategy would determine the nature of AML compliance in that industry.

Furthermore, this aggregate strategy in turn points to the nature of a regulatory environment. A regulatory environment where most MLROs are adopting the *discharging* strategy is conceptualised as *weak regulatory* environment since they are just playing along but not necessarily preventing money laundering. In a situation where the predominant strategy is *communicating*, the regulatory environment is called *tough regulation* since MLROs are compelled to challenge their organisations because of the pressure from regulators. In a situation where MLROs are predominantly *complying* with regulations because of fair pressure from regulators, the regulatory regime is called *smart regulation*. Finally, in a situation where MLROs are predominantly *cooperating* with the banks because of fair pressure from the banks, the regulatory environment is called *self-regulation*.

At the end, an approach was proposed that would make AML compliance more effective and efficient. The approach, called the *middle course approach*, identified a middle ground between *smart regulation* and *self-regulation* as a better strategy that would deal with the problem of ineffective enforcement associated with self-regulation and inefficient enforcement associated with *smart regulation*. This strategy is also good for banks in that it would be more efficient than *self-regulation* and more effective than *smart regulation*.

Potential Significance of the Book

By looking at the AML environment from the perspective of MLROs, it is hoped that the main problem relating to AML will be identified rather than a professional problem that is either dictated by regulators or promoted by banks. Following from this is the potential to show that MLROs, though part of the banking industry, are distinct individuals with different concerns from both the regulators and the banks. Understanding this difference may lead to a better understanding of the AML environment.

Most importantly, however, introducing a theory to AML literature has the potential of opening a new vista in AML research and practice because of the limited theoretical studies in the field. Thus, the theory can be a source for further research within the industry in addition to providing an explanation and prediction of compliance behaviour. The framework that was discovered and the subsequent recommended approach also have the potential to contribute to knowledge and practice.

Finally, the theory has potential for general implication in other substantive areas because it is well integrated with other theories, especially in economics, sociology and psychology.

Study Paradigm and Methodology

It is important to highlight the philosophy and methodology adopted for the research that gave birth to the book. This, however, is a summary of the process that led to the generation of the self-protecting theory.

Based on a suggestion in the literature, the author first identified his personal philosophical position on the nature of reality and knowledge. It was discovered that the author's position is aligned to a realist ontology and subjective epistemology. A range of literature on paradigm was then consulted to find out the paradigm that is closest to this position, and it was discovered that Pragmatism is the closest to the position of the author. However, Peirce Pragmatism is more closely aligned because of its explicit, realistic ontological position rather than other versions of Pragmatism that hold a more relativist position.

As a result of this choice, the methodology of enquiry was then narrowed to only those that support a realist ontological view. Others that have a relativist view were immediately rejected since the ontological position was considered the most important criteria for selecting a paradigm and invariably a methodology. Consequently, constructivism, social construction and other interpretive methodologies were not considered for the research. Among the methodology that supports a realist view, a second criterion was added, namely to find a methodology that aligns with the objective of the research.

Accordingly, classical grounded theory was identified as the closest methodology that satisfies the ontological question and provides procedures for answering the questions and objectives of the book. In addition, the methodology is well accepted, and leading approach in social research (Clarke & Friese 2007), it also provides a *"helpful framework for guiding data collection and analysis"* (McCann & Clark 2003 p. 16) and there is a *"wealth of literature on coding and analysis"* (Urquhart 2001 p. 14) that would make it easier to adopt. Unlike some methodologies, classical grounded theory is also a complete package that has procedures for data collection, analysis and even write-up (Elliott & Lazenbatt 2005; Glaser 1999).

Initially, the Strauss's version of grounded theory was considered because of its roots in Pragmatism, but it was discovered that its philosophical basis is more towards the relative pragmatic position and, therefore, inconsistent with the position of the author. It was the desire to achieve a *"methodological congruence"* in which it is important to match philosophy, methodology and method when conducting a study that mostly influence the choice of classical grounded theory over the Strauss and Corbin's approach.

Below is a summary of the procedures in classical grounded theory:

Misunderstood concepts in grounded theory

Before explaining the process, however, it is important to understand some key terms that relate to coding which are often misunderstood leading to failure of the coding process (Glaser 1998).

Concept

A concept is the idea that summarises the incident that is being analysed. Data can be from an interview or secondary data, but a concept is the word or phrase that is generated to represent an incident in the data. It can be a concept borrowed from the participants themselves, called *"in vivo code"* (Glaser 2008 p. 4), which they use to represent a set of data, or a word or a phrase generated by the researcher when coding the data. However it has been discovered that concepts *"are abstract of time, place, and people and that concepts have enduring grab"* (Glaser 2008 p. 3).

Category

A category is a concept that represents how participants are resolving their main concern (Glaser 1998). *"It captures the underlying patterns in the data"* (Glaser 1998 p. 135). A category is different from concerns of participants which can also be represented by a concept, but once it is called a category it is specifically referring to a concept that represents the way of resolving a concern, not the concern itself.

Furthermore, a category has different conceptual levels. There is the core, which is the *"highest level, then sub core, then categories for theoretical completeness"* (Glaser 1998 p. 135). According Glaser (2008 p. 15) the core is the category which *"organizes the other categories by continually resolving the main concern"*, while sub core categories are those that relate to the core category (Glaser 1998).

Property

A property is a concept about a category (Glaser 1998). It is a lower level concept than a category although *"some categories can also be considered properties of other categories"* (Glaser 1998 p. 136).

The following example from Glaser (1998 p. 135) explains the relationship better.

> Service people cultivate clients. Cultivating is a category. They cultivate for profit. Profit is a property of cultivating. They cultivate for cliental building. Cliental building is a property of cultivating. They cultivate up the social status and down the social status structure. The social status structure direction is a property of cultivating. They may cultivate for fun, referral etc. which are more properties of cultivating.

By understanding these three terms, coding in classical grounded theory is easy to understand and undertake.

Procedures in Classical Grounded Theory

There are certain sets of processes that must be followed when undertaking quality research (Jones & Noble 2007). These processes include theoretical sampling, memoing, saturation and substantive coding. Others are theoretical coding, theoretical sorting and theoretical writing. *"All are vital, necessary aspect of doing grounded theory"* (Glaser 1978 p. 2). The following section describes the processes.

Theoretical Sampling

"Theoretical sampling is the process of data collection for generating theory whereby the analyst jointly collects, codes, and analyzes his data and decides what data to collect next and where to find them, in order to discover his theory as it emerges". (Glaser & Strauss 1967 p. 45). It is, therefore, the process of sampling in which further data collection depends on analysis (Elliott & Lazenbatt 2005; Glaser 1978; Glaser 1998; Gurd 2008).

In a traditional qualitative research, a researcher usually has a clear view of the participants he is going to interview and the method of selecting those participants (Corbin & Strauss 1990). In addition, there are a range of sampling methods that can be used in research to arrive at a pool of potential participants (Denzin & Lincoln 2005). In grounded theory, however, the *"decisions about which data should be collected next are determined by the theory that is being constructed"* (Suddaby 2006 p. 634).

Finally, it is essential to note that theoretical sampling is not the same as selective sampling (Glaser 1978) or purposeful sampling (Elliott & Lazenbatt 2005). It is "*'where next' in collecting data, the 'for what' according to the codes, and the 'why' from the analysis in memos*" (Glaser 1998 p. 157).

Substantive Coding

There are two types of coding under substantive coding: open coding and selective coding.

Open Coding

The first type of coding is open coding. The goal of the researcher, according to Glaser (1978 p. 56), is *to "generate an emergent set of categories and their properties which fit, work and are relevant for integrating into a theory"*. Open coding is the first stage of that process in which data is analysed in order to discover concepts. In other words, it is *"running the data open"* (Glaser 1978 p. 56) or a process "by which data are broken down analytically" (Corbin & Strauss 1990 p. 12).

For a successful open coding process, the following questions should be kept in mind: *"what is the data a study of? What category does this incident indicate? What is actually happening in the data?"* (Glaser 1978 p. 57). These questions "*keep the analyst theoretically sensitive and transcending when analysing, collecting and coding his data. They force him to focus on patterns among incidents which yield codes, and to rise conceptualisation above fascinating experiences*" (Glaser 1978 p. 57). For Glaser (1998 p. 141), these questions were further simplified to "*what category does this incident indicate?", "what property of what category does this incident indicate?" and lastly "what is the participant's main concern?"*.

Another essential procedure in open coding is to *"analyse the data line by line"* (Glaser 1978 p. 57). This means that each line is read, and a concept is generated or adopted. Subsequent coding would then follow, but no new code is generated until the researcher is satisfied that existing codes do not cover that incident – this is the process of constant comparison introduced earlier. In its basic form, constant comparison means that *"while coding an incident for a category, compare it with the previous incidents in the same and different groups coded in the same category"* (Glaser & Strauss 1967 p. 106). In other words, a researcher first *"compares incident to incident, then as a category or its property emerges, he compares the concept to the next incident"* (Glaser 1998 p. 139).

Selective Coding

When open coding is completed and a core category is identified, further data collection and analysis will be focused towards the core and its related categories (Jones & Noble 2007). This process of coding for core category is called selective coding (Corbin & Strauss 1990; Glaser 1978). It is a process *"by which all categories are unified around a 'core' category"* (Corbin & Strauss 1990 p. 14). It means that the *"analyst delimits his coding to only those variables that relate to the core variable in sufficiently significant ways to be used in a parsimonious theory"* (Glaser 1978 p. 61). It does not mean, however; that other categories are ignored. What it means is that the focus henceforth would be on the chosen core while other categories are viewed in relation to that core (Glaser 1978).

The coding process in both open and selective coding stages are, however, the same except that it is not necessary to do a line by line coding during the selective coding process. This much was emphasised by Glaser (2011 p. 75) when he stated: "*DO NOT keep coding the data for a code that has saturated or is unrelated to the core. Thus soon, skipping and dipping occurs and one can pass on lots of collected data since it adds nothing but more incidents to already saturated codes"*.

Theoretical Saturation

Theoretical saturation is another concept of grounded theory that means a point is reached when no further data collection would add anything new to conceptualisation (Suddaby 2006). In the words of Glaser and Strauss (1967 p. 61) it *"means that no additional data are being found whereby the sociologist can discover properties of the category. As he sees similar instances over and over again, the researcher becomes empirically confident that a category is saturated"*.

The transition between open coding to selective coding can, however, be difficult if not frightening for some researcher (Allan, 2003; Glaser, 1998). *"How does the analyst know when it is safe to selectively code for a core variable and to cease open coding?"* (Glaser 1978 p. 61). Thankfully, there are some criteria to apply for assessing whether a core category has emerged, details of which can found in Glaser (1978). Some of these criteria include: *"core category must be central…, it must reoccur frequently in the data…, it relates meaningfully and easily with other categories… It is completely variable and it can be any kind of theoretical code"* (Glaser 1978 p. 96).

Theoretical Coding

In this stage, coding is focused towards integrating categories according to a theoretical code. Theoretical codes are codes that serve as models for discovering theories (Glaser & Holton 2005). *"They, like substantive codes are emergent; they weave the fractured story back together. Without substantive code, they are empty abstractions"* (Glaser 1978 p. 72). Theoretical coding is therefore *"categorizing empirical data on the basis of previous theoretical knowledge"* (Kelle 2005 p. 10).

There are several established codes, as will be discussed later in the section, but a researcher can still discover as many as possible and select the one that best fits the categories and their properties in the emerging theory (Glaser 1978). Some of the codes can even come from other disciplines totally unrelated to the substantive area (Glaser 1978; Glaser 2005; Glaser & Holton 2005); the paramount consideration is to have a theoretical code that binds the core category, its property and related categories into a theory that fits, that works and is relevant.

The most common example of a theoretical code is the six C coding family (Glaser 1978), which stands for Causes, Context, Contingencies, Consequences, Covariance and Conditions. Other families of theoretical codes include the process and degree families (Glaser 1978; Glaser 1998); binary, balancing and cross pressure (Glaser 2005); and paired opposite and scale families (Glaser 1998).

Theoretical Memoing

This is another essential part of grounded theory (Corbin & Strauss 1990). In fact, it is "*the bedrock of theory generation*" (Glaser 1978 p. 83), without which a "*great deal of conceptual detail is lost or left undiscovered*" (Corbin & Strauss 1990 p. 10). A theoretical memo is a memo about concepts and the relationship between them or in more technical terms, "*memos are the theorizing write-up of ideas about substantive codes and their theoretically coded relationship as the emerge during coding, collecting and analysing data and during memo*" (Glaser 1998 p. 177). It is the "*write-up of ideas about codes and their relationship as they strike the analyst while coding*" (Glaser 1978 p. 83). In theoretical memoing, a researcher writes a memo about the category or its property; how it was discovered, its relations with previous concept, the ideas attached to it, the similarities and difference between concepts, but making sure to avoid description, because memoing is a "*theorizing write up*" not a detailed description.

In summary, the aim of memoing is to achieve the following five aspects of generating theory in that it,

> raises the data to a conceptual level, discovers the property of each category which begins to define it operationally, presents hypothesis about connections between categories and/or their properties, begins to integrate these connections with clusters of or other categories to generate the theory and begins to locate the emerging theory with other theories with potentially more or less relevance. (Glaser 1978 p. 84)

Another important function of a memo is to check the researcher's bias (Elliott & Lazenbatt 2005). By constantly comparing incident to incidents; concept to concepts and writing evolving ideas into a memo, the researcher's bias is challenged (Corbin & Strauss 1990; Glaser 2002). In grounded theory, therefore, the issue of subjectivity is addressed through the twin concepts of memoing and constant comparison just as studies in qualitative research and phenomenology use reflexivity and bracketing respectively (Elliott & Lazenbatt 2005).

Theoretical Sorting

Theoretical sorting occurs towards the end of the process when categories are almost saturated, and when a memo bank is matured (Glaser 1998). It is based on memos stored in the memo bank from where they are taken and sorted to form a theory. It is still important to continue saturating categories and gathering data as needed, but they are necessarily not as important as in previous stages because during this stage *"the researcher is exhausted and saturated, physical, temporally and financially. Theoretical sampling no longer seems relevant"* (Glaser 1998 p. 188). Memos are, however, still generated during sorting (Glaser 2012) to refine categories and document emerging theory.

Theoretical sorting not only facilitates the emergence of a theoretical code but it also arranges memos according to that emerged theoretical code (Glaser 2012). The theoretical decision, for example, of *"the precise location of a particular memo – as the analyst sees similarities, connections and underlying uniformities – is based on the theoretical coding of the data that is grounding the idea"* (Glaser 1978 p. 118).

Similarly, sorting involves arranging memos in relation to a core category (Glaser 2012). This process of arranging memos was demonstrated by Strauss and Corbin (1990 p. 238) as *"reading and rereading them, and then by sorting them, we can begin to discover how the categories come together around a core category"*. Sorting is, therefore, essential for discovering a theory (Glaser 1998; Strauss & Corbin 1990); it is also a great source of material for presentations and discussions (Glaser 1978); and it is better done manually.

In summary, the process of sorting is best described as follows:

> At the start the researcher faces virtually a large pile of memo. He should enter the pile anywhere, no matter where and pick up a memo. He/she then places the memo anywhere on a table which should be large, like a dining table so it will spatially accommodate the coming piles. Then he picks up another memo, compares it to the first memo and does a brief memo about how it relates to the first memo and start another pile. (Glaser 2012 p. 42)

It is, however, important to remember that sorting is *"of ideas, not data, it is a conceptual sorting, not data sorting. Unlike data sorting, where 'hired hands' are acceptable, conceptual sorting requires that the analyst do his own work. Only he knows his concepts well enough and has the sensitivity to determine how they may relate to other ideas to be integrated into a theory"* (Glaser 1978 p. 116).

Theoretical Writing

The final stage of grounded theory methodology after theoretical sorting is theoretical writing (Glaser 1978). The idea *"is to write-up the piles of sorted memos (called sorts)"* (Glaser 1998 p. 193) in order to communicate the theory to readers. Writing in classical grounded theory is not a difficult process because the materials are already available; what is required is to recall them from the sorted memos and make them comprehensible (Glaser 1998; Strauss & Corbin, 1990).

Writing in grounded theory is an integral part of the methodology since classical grounded theory is a complete package (Elliott & Lazenbatt 2005; Glaser 1999). Consequently, this study followed the suggestions in classical grounded theory books especially Stop, Write (Glaser 2012) and Theoretical Sensitivity (Glaser 1978) in writing the theory section of the book.

The key to writing a grounded theory is for a write up to have *"logic of construction, of shape and conceptual style"* (Glaser 1978 p. 129). Construction depends on "little logic" which is *"a carefully, grounded, systematic emergent construction job on how a core category continually accounts for the variability on resolving a main concern"* (Glaser 2012 p. 62). It is a statement that shows how the core category explains the behaviour of participants in the substantive area (Glaser 1978).

The shape of a grounded theory study is not unlike other studies. It begins with introducing the *"core category and at most 3, sub concepts and how they resolve the main concern"* (Glaser 2012 p. 60). The main concern is, however, not derived from the literature as in other qualitative research (Glaser 2002), but it emerges from the data by following the procedures of grounded theory. The main body of the write up is based on the emerging theoretical code which provides the outline for writing the theory (Glaser 2012). The concluding part of the write-up contains information about the implication of the theory, its use, contribution and recommendation (Glaser 2012). Recommendation is particularly important to show the relevance of the theory to practice (Glaser 1978).

On the style of the write up, the *"dictum is to write conceptually, by making theoretical statements about relationships between concepts, rather than writing descriptive statement about people"* (Glaser 1978 p. 133). Descriptive statement can, however, be included, but only as illustrations (Glaser 1978) and *"they should be kept to a minimum"* (Glaser 2012 p. 69). It is not the goal of grounded theory to prove the theory,

> The credibility of the theory should be won by its integration, relevance and workability, not illustrations used as if it were proof. The assumption of the reader, he should be advised, is that all concepts are grounded and that the massive grounding effort could not be shown in writing. Also that as grounded they are not proven: they are only suggestions. The theory is an integrated set of hypothesis, not findings. (Glaser 1978 p. 134)

Literature is later woven into the theory to show the bigger picture (Glaser 2012; McCann & Clark 2003; Urquhart 2001). Literature review by the researcher is, however, not used to *"find in the literature an idea he has generated, especially in the literature of great men"* (Glaser 1978 p. 137). Using the literature is, therefore, to provide *"integrative placement"* (Glaser 2012 p. 103), which means including literature in the text to indicate how the emerging theory fits other theories relating to the core category. This is essential because *"true scholarly incorporation of literature will ground his theory in the literature and will legitimate even more the grounded theory as a contribution to a substantive area"* (Glaser 1998 p. 207). *"It is a travesty not to do this scholarly work"* (Glaser 2012 p. 101).

Ethical Issues

Ethics is a topical subject and an important part of conducting research. The need for ethics became apparent after the serious unethical practices of the past came to light. Some of the practices included a study on syphilis, between 1932 to 1972, when 400 African American people were left untreated for syphilis in order to study the disease. Another example was the treatment of pregnant women in the 1950s with a medicine that had serious side effects including cancer (Orb et al. 2001). Although these practices were prevalent mainly in quantitative research, there are also instances of unethical research practices in qualitative research (Punch 1994). As a result of these practices and in order to protect the integrity of research, several requirements were set for conducting research. These included fair treatment of research participants, confidentiality, anonymity, duty of care and integrity.

In order to avoid these ethical issues, the author obtained ethical approval for the study and strictly adhered to the provisions of the approval. Before an interview, for example, an informed consent form was sent to participants for their consent. Participants sometimes returned the completed consent forms before the interview or they gave their consent through an email and then signed the consent form before or after the interview.

Furthermore, interviews were not recorded to ensure confidentiality and anonymity and to adhere to the tenets of the classical grounded theory. For each interview, however, a field note was written immediately after the interview. Similarly, each interview lasted for forty five minutes at most to ensure that participants were not inconvenienced. They were also allowed to select a location for the interview to ensure confidentiality.

The use of grounded theory also ensured that some ethical ensures were minimised. The requirement not to tape interviews, for example, greatly reduced the likelihood of a breach of confidentiality. Data was also soon conceptualised as it was collected with further analysis mainly conducted on analysed data in the form of memos rather than the actual data. In addition, when presenting the theory for the research, extensive data from the participants was not used, in line with the methodology, thereby reducing the risk of unintentional breach of confidentiality and anonymity.

Finally, all efforts were taken to ensure that data was kept confidential. Hand copies of consent forms and field notes were kept in a locked cupboard while soft copies were kept in a password-protected network. The author also ensured that field notes were not available to anybody apart from the author and his supervision team. Snippets of data are, however, included in the book and may be used later when presenting the research, but the names of participants and organisations were anonymised to avoid a breach of confidentiality.

Outline of the Book

The book comprises seven chapters, which are described below:

Chapter 1

Introduction

There has been a lot of discussion about the level of effectiveness of AML within the UK and even globally. Some have attributed the problem with AML to weak regulatory and compliance framework, others lay the blame on the regulated sector for not doing enough to prevent money laundering, while some have attributed the problem to the cost of compliance imposed by the regulators. This book looks at the problem of AML from the perspective of one of the most important stakeholders, that is, the MLRO, because their voice is often not heard in the debate despite the critical role they play in AML.

Consequently, the chapter introduces the problem with AML from the perspective of MLROs. The aims and objectives of the research, the justification of the study and a brief discussion on the philosophy and methodology adopted for the research are also included in the chapter.

Chapter 2

Background of the AML Environment

This chapter provides a background and context to the research. It starts with the history of anti-money laundering (AML) compliance, tracing the first formal regulation on AML compliance to the current system of risk-based approach. The role of international organisations in the development of AML was also discussed before focusing on the UK regulatory environment as the focus of the study. Finally, the role of MLROs was discussed in relation to AML compliance.

Chapter 3

The Self-protecting Theory—A Theory of MLROs

This chapter presents the *self-protecting* theory discovered in the research. The theory explains how MLROs are dealing with their main concern of *unfair pressure*. The main concern is discussed and then the *protecting* behaviour for resolving it followed. Before then, however, a section is presented explaining the major entities related to the theory (banks, regulators and MLROs) to provide context for understanding the process of conceptualisation leading to the discovery of the theory.

A section is then included that shows the details of how the theory emerged using the classical grounded theory techniques adopted for the research. At the end, the self-protecting framework discovered from the theory is discussed to show the potential contribution of the theory.

Chapter 4

Compliance and Regulatory Dilemma

This chapter reviews the literature on regulation in general and then relates it to AML regulation and compliance. Essentially, the problem of regulation and compliance is to find the right balance between the effectiveness of regulation and the efficiency of compliance. Economic, social and socioeconomic theories of regulation were reviewed to explore the problem and situate the discussion within the context of AML.

Chapter 5

The Potential Solution to the Dilemma

The *self-protecting* theory is essentially a theory of regulation. It explains how MLROs balance the desire of regulators to have an effective regulation and the desire of banks to have an efficient compliance. The chapter presents the Middle Course Approach, a potential solution to the effectiveness and efficiency trade-off. The approach was discovered from the *self- protecting* framework which suggests that for an effective and efficient AML regulation and compliance, MLROs should be treated fairly and given the required independence to perform their function of implementing AML regulations.

Chapter 6

General Application of the Self-protecting Theory

Although it is evident that the contribution of the self-protecting theory has been established because a theory was discovered to explain the protecting behaviour of MLROs and a recommendation was provided for an effective and efficient AML, it is, however, important to make the contribution more explicit by relating the theory to other substantive areas where it could be applicable.

Following the advice of Urquhart (2013), the contribution is illustrated using Walsham's analytical generalisation framework (Walsham 1995) in which a theoretical contribution is illustrated using four ways namely: development of concepts, generation of theory, drawing specific implication and contributing to rich insights.

Chapter 7

Conclusion

This chapter presents the conclusion of the book. It starts by summarising the emergent theory of self-protecting and the key concepts that make up the theory. The theory that was presented in Chap. 3 essentially states that the more pressure exerted on MLROs, the more they protect themselves rather than preventing money laundering. This theory was used to develop a framework that is potentially able to assess any AML environment to determine its effectiveness and efficiency. The solution discussed in Chap. 5 to the problem of striking a balance between the effectiveness of regulation and the efficiency of compliance was also highlighted.

The theoretical and methodological contributions of the research are also discussed as well as the significance of the study. The chapter also presents how the aims and objectives of the research were achieved before finally discussing the limitation of the study and the implication for future research.

Conclusion

The focus in this book is on MLROs within the UK banking industry. The chapter, therefore, started by providing a background on the environment in which they operate and introduced the purpose and justification for writing the book. Furthermore, one of the motivations for this book is the opportunity to contribute to knowledge by introducing a theory within the AML area. Thus, throughout the study underpinning the book, the questions presented in this chapter guided the discovery of a theory that works and is relevant.

2

Background of the AML Environment

Introduction

This chapter provides a background and context for the book. The chapter is, therefore, not meant to be a literature review of the substantive area, but a brief summary of the anti-money laundering (AML) environment. It starts with the history of AML compliance, tracing the first formal regulation on AML compliance to the current system of risk-based approach, which is the current system of operation in the United Kingdom (UK). Accordingly, the legal framework for AML in the UK is discussed. The role of international organisations in the development of AML will also be highlighted before focusing on the UK regulatory environment as the focus of the study.

Finally, the role of money laundering reporting officers (MLROs) is discussed in relation to AML compliance since the book is about finding out the main concern of MLROs and how they are resolving it.

A.U. Bello, *Improving Anti-Money Laundering Compliance*,
Palgrave Studies in Risk, Crime and Society,
DOI 10.1007/978-3-319-43264-9_2

History of Anti-Money Laundering

There is no consensus on the origin of the term "money laundering". Some researchers have traced the origin of the term to the practice of washing coins in casinos to make sure they did not spoil the white gloves of the casino ladies (Unger 2013b), while, in other places, it was traced to the time of Al Capone who used to launder his criminal proceeds using launderette to avoid detection by law enforcement (Unger 2013b). There are also some who traced its origin to the Watergate scandal, when it first appeared in newspapers (Schneider & Windischbauer 2008). What is certain, however, is the definition of the term which, in its simplest form, means the process of disguising the origin of illicit money to make it appear legitimate (Ryder 2012) or the illicit transfer of money to hide its true origin (Takats 2011; Unger 2013b).

Stages of Money Laundering

Money laundering has three stages: placement, layering and integration (Reuter & Truman 2004). Placement is the first stage of the process where a money launderer introduces his illicit funds into a legitimate system by disguising its origin. Once the money is in the system, he will then initiate a complex web of transactions to further disguise the source of the money, distancing it as far as possible from its source in a process called layering. And finally, once the money has been sufficiently distanced from its origin, it is integrated into the economy as if it is from a legitimate source. At this last stage of integration, it is usually difficult to identify the activities as money laundering transactions.

Effect of Money Laundering

Even though the practice of money laundering has apparently been around since ancient times (Unger 2013a), it was not unit 1986 that that it was criminalised (Sharman 2008). The main reason for criminalising it is because of the impact it has on the society especially in the early years when money laundering was largely synonymous with drug trafficking (FATF 2012). One of the effects of money laundering is its threat to the legal economy (Barone & Masciandaro 2011). Money laundering can also *"undermine the integrity and stability of financial institutions and systems, discourage foreign investment, and distort international capital flows"* (Tanzi 1996 p. 1). Other effects, according to Unger and van der Linde (2013), include economic, social and political effects of money laundering. The economic effect involves unfair competition, price distortion and negative effect on investments. On the social side, they stated that it encourages corruption and bribery since disguising the origin of money may require compromising those that are responsible for operating a legitimate system of money transfer. The political effect is centred around having criminals using their ill-gotten money to gain political power and in the process further corrupting the system by laundering the proceeds of their crimes.

Although it is believed that the effect of money laundering is huge (Barone & Masciandaro 2011), at least in the estimation of regulatory authorities (Harvey 2008), it is, however, difficult to estimate the actual extent of the effect on the economy (Barone & Masciandaro 2011; Harvey 2009; Ryder 2008; Unger & Busuioc 2007) despite the "courageous attempts" (Unger & Busuioc, 2007 p. 29) that have been made to estimate the magnitude of the problem. There are various studies that have tried to measure the impact, but according Masciandaro and Barone (2008 p. 9), *"most literature on ML effects is pure speculation, or it is based on figures that are either wrongly cited, misinterpreted or just invented"*. An example of this is an estimate by the IMF in 2001 which stated that the annual amount of money laundering was in the region of 2–5% of the world's GDP (Schroeder 2001). Other estimates include a study in 1995 the puts that amount of money laundered globally at US$2.85 trillion (Walker & Unger 2009). These two estimates, although popular in the literature, are considered doubtful because the methodologies used to estimate the amounts are not replicable (Barone & Masciandaro 2011; Schneider & Windischbauer 2008). This is mainly because the IMF has not explained how they arrived at the estimate, and the Walker's model also lacks adequate disclosure (Masciandaro & Barone 2008). Despite this reservation, however, it is agreed that money laundering has a negative effect on the economy even if the extent of the effect is not quantifiable (Barone & Masciandaro 2011). The challenge is, therefore, to find a methodology that would be able to provide a reliable estimate of the extent of money laundering (Harvey 2009).

Objectives of AML

As a result of the threat of money laundering to the economy and the financial system (FATF 2012; Schott 2006), the international community set as an objective the protection of the society from its effect (Ross & Hannan 2007). Not everybody, however, agrees with the purpose of AML as promoted by the regulatory authorities (Harvey & Lau 2009). Furthermore, the terrorist event of 9–11 brought to the fore another purpose of AML which is to prevent terrorists from exploiting the financial system to commit terrorism (FATF 2012). Anti-terrorism is an important part of AML regulation because terrorism and money laundering are closely related. According to Cassella (2004), for example, terrorism is an example of reverse money laundering where criminals launder clean money to commit crimes in the future.

To achieve the purposes of AML, governments across the world adopted two strategies: firstly, directly introducing harsh policies against money launderers through efforts on predicate offences, and secondly, introducing preventive policies to make sure that the proceeds of crime are not laundered through regulated entities (van den Broek 2011). Law enforcement agencies were left with their traditional responsibility of investigating and prosecuting the predicate offence of money laundering while regulated entities were primarily charged with the responsibility of preventing money laundering by ensuring that they have adequate systems and controls to prevent the use of their systems for laundering the proceeds of crime (Araujo 2008).

Among the regulated entities, banks are the first and the most important entities charged with the responsibilities of prevention of money laundering (Shehu 2005) since one of the main methods for laundering money is through the international financial system (Geiger & Wuensch 2007) and since bank transfer is the main method of facilitating money laundering (Takats 2011).

Initially, banks were reluctant to comply with regulations on AML because of the conflict between AML and other organisational objectives *"especially when it comes to communicating information concerning dubious dealings and defining relations with the public regulatory agencies"* (Favarel-Garrigues et al. 2008 p. 9), since according to Canhoto (2008 p. 167) *"ultimately, AML runs against the traditional ethos as well as the strategic objectives of banks"*. Banks were, however, forced to cooperate, especially after the events of 9–11, which changed the approach to the fight against money laundering (Favarel-Garrigues et al. 2011). Banks were, therefore, left with no option but to comply, but because of the conflict mentioned above, their focus became one of protecting themselves against regulatory risk and not necessarily the risk of money laundering (Favarel-Garrigues et al. 2011).

It is not only the financial sector that is required to comply with the AML regulations; countries and jurisdictions were also implicitly required to comply with the Financial Action Task Force (FATF) Recommendations because of the negative impact that non-compliance would have on their jurisdiction even though the Recommendations are not binding (Shehu 2005). In 2001, for example, the FATF introduced the Non-cooperative Countries and Territories list (NCCT) that designated certain countries as non-cooperative. The impact of this designation was to impose harsh measures for dealing with an NCCT country including *"FATF-member countries terminating transactions with financial institutions from such a country"* (Schott 2006 p. 111–11). This practice was, however, discontinued in 2006 when the last of the NCCT countries were delisted (FATF 2007a). There is, however, a similar list of high risks and non-cooperative jurisdictions for countries having strategic AML deficiencies which the FATF is supporting to address the deficiencies (FATF 2013b). Others that are also required to comply with AML regulations, by the UK's Money Laundering Regulations, for example, include lawyers, accountants, money transmission service, bureaux de change, real estate agents and dealers in high-value goods (Rhodes & Palastrand 2004; Sproat 2007). The fourth AML Directive has extended the scope even further to cover more crimes and additional professions and activities (European Union 2015).

The argument for the drive toward preventative action is largely because of the belief that AML has an inverse relationship with money laundering (Masciandaro 1999; Sathye & Islam 2011). There are, however, others that do not believe that the AML regime is effective in reducing money laundering (Demetis & Angell 2007). This argument may be supported giving that the financial system is only one of the options for laundering money, albeit an important one. Other options, according to Geiger and Wuensch (2007), include money launderers keeping their cash, circulating it within the criminal world so there is no need of laundering, and using Hawala-type transactions that do not necessarily require the use of a financial system in order to operate. Even for financial and designated non-financial institutions that are subject to much regulation, a money launderer can evade the system because of the ineffectiveness of AML regulations as documented in some studies (Demetis & Angell 2007; Killick & Parody 2007; Rhodes & Palastrand 2004).

International Regulations

Although AML effort started in the United States (US) in the 1970s with the introduction of the Bank Secrecy Act (Dolar & Shughart II 2011; Reuter & Truman 2004), it was not until 1988 that significant global efforts for AML regulation began with the adoption of the UN Convention against the Illicit Traffic in Narcotic Drugs and Psychotropic Substances in Vienna (Ryder 2008; Shehu 2005). The Convention was, therefore, the first international instrument developed to deal with money laundering through its provisions for the identification, seizure and confiscation of the proceeds of crime (UNODC 2013c). Although money laundering was not specifically mentioned in the Convention, it was, however, the basis on which subsequent AML regulations were built (Stessens 2000).

United Nations (UN)

Subsequent initiatives were introduced by the UN to fight money laundering and it predicated offences. The first of these initiatives was the Global Programme against Money Laundering, established in 1997 to give effect to some of the provisions of the UN Convention against the Illicit Traffic in Narcotic Drugs and Psychotropic Substances (UNODC 2013a). The objective of the programme *"is to strengthen the ability of Member States to implement measures against money-laundering and the financing of terrorism and to assist them in detecting, seizing and confiscating illicit proceeds"* (UNODC 2013a).

International Money-Laundering Information Network (IMoLIN) and Anti-Money-Laundering International Database (AMLID) were also established in 1998 to provide information about money laundering laws and regulations in member countries and to facilitate international cooperation (UNODC 2013b). The information on IMoLIN, for example, is available free on the internet for all type of users, but the AMLID is a secure database for restricted use.

As a result of the inadequacy of the 1988 Convention due to its limited support for international cooperation (Shehu 2005), a UN Convention against Transnational Organised Crime was introduced in 2000 to widen the scope of predicated offences for money laundering to include not only drug offences, but all serious crimes (UNODC 2013c). A separate convention became necessary because of the seriousness of corruption as a global problem (United Nations 2004) and the inadequacy of the previous conventions to deal with it (Shehu 2005).

Hence, the UN Convention against Corruption was introduced in 2003 to promote measures against corruption, to support international cooperation and to promote integrity. Another initiative related to money laundering is the International Convention for the Suppression of the Financing of Terrorism that came into force in 2002 which seek to protect the financial system from being used for terrorism purposes (UNODC 2013c).

The main problem with these UN conventions according to Shehu (2005), however, is that UN agreements are by consensus, so there is necessarily going to be a compromise whenever a decision is to be taken. UN initiatives also mostly reflect the concerns of stronger nations while the priorities of weaker nations are usually ignored (Shehu 2005). An example was given by Shehu (2005) who stated that Turkey and Egypt were at the forefront of the campaign for terrorism convention in the UN assembly before 2001, but it was not until after 9–11 that the issue was given the seriousness that it deserved because on its impact on the

US, one of the most powerful members of that organisation. Before then, however, the International Convention for the Suppression of the Financing of Terrorism was introduced in 1999 to enhance international co-operation and to prevent terrorism.

Financial Action Task Force (FATF)

It was also in 1988 that AML was institutionalised. This happened as a result of a meeting of the group of seven most industrialised nations (G7) in Paris, which led to the formation of the FATF to coordinate the global fight agent money laundering (FATF 2013c). The creation of the FATF and its subsequent establishment of the 40 Recommendations in 1989 was considered *"the most comprehensive, multidimensional and multisectoral approach in the global efforts to combat ml"* (Shehu 2005 p. 232). It was the most significant because it provided specific requirements, included the private sector fully in the AML effort, defined the role of regulatory authorities, and provided a framework for its implementation (FATF 1990). The 40 Recommendations are also accepted worldwide with 188 countries using them (FATF 2013a).

The specific nature of the 40 Recommendations was the basis of the rule-based approach to AML (Yan et al. 2011) that was later shown to be ineffective as contained in a review by van den Broek (2011). The recommendations contain requirements that member countries are obliged to follow to assist in the global fight against money laundering. Some of the requirements include a threshold for currency reporting (van den Broek 2011), know your customer requirements and suspicious activity reporting (Jackson 2000).

As a result of the implementation of the 40 Recommendations, concerns were raised especially by the regulated entities about the cost of compliance and the additional burden of fulfilling the requirements (Geiger & Wuensch 2007; Rhodes & Palastrand 2004). The KYC requirements for example were considered time consuming, intrusive and has no effect on reducing money laundering (Edwards & Wolfe 2005). These and similar concerns led to the revision of the 40

Recommendations in 2003 to allow for a risk based approach to compliance (de Koker 2009; Ross & Hannan 2007), but it was not until 2007 that the risk based approach was made more explicit in the FATF guidance notes (FATF 2007b).

Part of the revision undertaken in 2003 included the expansion in the definition of financial institution, a focus on Politically Exposed Persons (PEP), expansion of laws, inclusion of gatekeepers as regulated entities and the introduction of a system of mutual assessment of member countries (Shehu 2005). The 2003 revision and similar exercises were, however, criticised for expanding the scope of predicate offences and transferring additional responsibilities to banks who are not well equipped to handle them (Geiger & Wuensch 2007).

The 2003 revision was, however, not the only revision to the first set of 40 Recommendations. Due to the increasing threat of terrorism and in response to the 9–11 attacks in the US, the FATF, in 2001 and 2004, added nine special recommendations specifically to deal with the financing of terrorism (FATF 2005). Later in 2012, the standards were further reviewed to include proliferation of weapons of mass destruction and the integration of the nine special recommendations into the original 40 Recommendations (FATF 2012).

Other International Best Practices

Other initiatives were also introduced following the start of the international focus on money laundering. The Basel Committee, World Bank and IMF are some of the institutions that were active during these periods.

Basel Committee on Banking Supervision

The Basel Committee introduced a similar initiative in 1988 to the forty Recommendations focusing on customer identification, compliance with laws and cooperation with law enforcement authorities (Basel 1988). Other similar initiatives by the Committee include the Consolidated KYC Risk Management (Basel 2004) and Customer Due Diligence

(Basel 2001). Their recommendations are, however, not laws but statements of principle to which banks are expected to adhere (Schott 2006).

World Bank and IMF

The involvement of the World Bank and the IMF was mainly in the form of providing technical assistance and joint assessment of member countries on the basis of the FATF's methodology (FATF 2012; Levi & Reuter 2006). A significant contribution of the two organisations is the production of a reference guidance to AML and the financing of terrorism in 2003, which is "*a single, comprehensive source of practical information for countries to fight money laundering and terrorist financing*" (Schott 2006 p. ix).

Egmont Group

The Egmont Group initiative is another contribution to the fight against money laundering. The Egmont Group is a group of financial intelligence units around the world that came together in 1995 to share intelligence and support each other with regards to AML (Egmont Group 2012). FIU are competent authorities set by various governments that collect, collate and disseminate intelligence both within and outside their jurisdictions for the purpose of preventing money laundering (Levi & Reuter 2006; Schott 2006). Part of their contribution include the publication of a sanitised report of 100 cases of money laundering from their members to share experiences with members and the general public (Egmont Group 2000).

Wolfsberg Group

The Wolfsberg initiative is yet another international effort by some of the major banks in the world as a reaction to the several global initiatives on money laundering. The Group, which came together in 2000, is now an association of 11 global banks with the aim of developing standards to deal with money laundering (Wolfsberg Group 2012). The main purpose of the Group was initially to provide anti-money laundering guideline for the private banking but they later expanded the scope to include provisions of guidance on terrorist financing, correspondent banking and the risk-based approach to AML among others (Wolfsberg Group 2014). In general, the aim of the Group is to develop policies and procedures that prevent the use of banks for criminal activities and to safeguard their reputation (Wolfsberg Group 2012).

Unlike other AML initiatives, this is a private sector led initiative which if implemented would make a significant contribution to the fight against money laundering (Hinterseer 2001). Others have criticised the implementation of the principles as ineffective due to the lack of *"specific enforcement mechanism"* (Shehu 2005 p. 241).

EU Legislative Measures

Following the Council of Europe Convention in 1988 the EU issued its first Directive in 1991 to implement the provision of the FATF 40 Recommendations, and in 2001 the Directive was amended to broaden the scope to include non-financial institutions as part of the regulated sector (Mitsilegas & Gilmore 2007). The Directives were essentially issued to prevent the use of financial system for the purpose of money laundering and the financing of terrorism (European Union 1991, 2001). Later, a third Directive (European Union 2005) was issued to replace the first two, and it became the most important tool in the fight against money laundering (European Union 2013).

The first two Directives were based on the rule-based approach, but with the introduction of the risk based approach in 2003 by the FATF, the third Directive brought the EU's regulations in line with the principle based approach (van den Broek 2011). Although members of the EU are obliged to follow these Directives, their implementation is, however, not harmonised, with various member countries partially adopting them to suite their existing regulations (van den Broek 2011).

The Directives, however, imposed further obligations on financial institutions especially as regard reporting requirements by including *"all those infractions punishable by more than a year in prison, including tax fraud*" (Favarel-Garrigues et al. 2008 p. 13). The implementation of the directives may also lead to a potential breach of civil liberties and fundamental rights of citizens given the zeal with which the EU is implementing the FATF's standard on money laundering and terrorist financing (Mitsilegas & Gilmore 2007). These breaches could include delay in the carriage of passengers and baggage covered by the Warsaw Convention.

The 4th AML Directive was, however, introduced to provide more clarity and to facilitate easier interpretation of the requirements of the Directives (European Union 2015).

The UK Regulatory Environment

The United Kingdom (UK) was in the forefront of implementation of the various Directives especially its progressive implementation of the risk based approach (de Koker 2009). As a result of this proactive approach, several laws have been enacted including Proceeds of Crime Act 2002 (POCA 2002), Serious Organised Crime and Police Act 2005 (SOCPA 2005), three Money Laundering Regulations (MLRs) (Ryder 2008). Prior to these Acts, the main AML legislation was provided by the Drug Trafficking Offences Act 1986 (DTA 1986), Criminal Justice Act 1988 (CJA 1988) and Terrorism Act 2000 (TA 2000) (JMLSG 2011). There was also the Court and Crimes Act 2013 that created the NCA.

The Treasury Department

In the UK, H.M. Treasury is responsible for policies related to financial services including money laundering (Bergstrom et al. 2011). It provides "*overall co-ordination of UK AML/CFT policy with the Home Office*" (FATF 2007c). There is, however, a strong private sector involvement through the Joint Money Laundering Steering Group (JMLSG), an organisation made of up the leading trade associations in the financial services sector with the aim of providing guidance to regulated entities in fulfilling their AML obligations (JMLSG 2014). The actual regulation of money laundering is, however, conducted by the Financial Conduct Authority (FCA), an agency that replaced the Financial Services Authority(FSA) (Financial Conduct Authority 2013a).

Financial Conduct Authority/Financial Services Authority

The FSA for the most part of the AML compliance period was the agency that was responsible for implementing various regulations related to money laundering. It was created in 1997 to regulate the financial industry following the enactment of the Financial Services and Market Act 2000 (Ryder 2008). AML oversight was given to the Authority through the provisions of s. 146 of the Act with the principal objective of ensuring that banks have adequate systems and controls to help prevent money laundering. The FSA was also given the powers to prosecute violators of money laundering regulations by the provision of s. 402 of that Act. These powers include power to prosecute for money laundering offences even if they fall outside the remit of the Financial Services and Markets Act 2000 (FSMA) as determined in R. v. Rollins [2010] UKSC 39.

The FSA initially enforced its regulations through a handbook that contains specific rules and regulations regarding money laundering. The use of the handbook was, however, phased out in 2006 partly because of the complaint of the onerous duties it imposed on the regulated sector, and was replaced by Senior Management Arrangements, Systems and Controls (SYSC), a principle-based guide to regulation (Ryder 2008).

Although it had the power of enforcement and prosecution, the FSA hardly used those powers except in some few high profile cases (Ryder 2008). It, however, has used its powers to impose penalties. Examples of recent cases include Coutts (£8.75m fine in March 2012); Habib Bank AG Zurich (£525,000 fine in May 2012); Turkish Bank (UK) Ltd (£294,000 fine in August 2012); and EFG Private Bank (£4.2m fine in April 2013) all for weakness in AML-control (Financial Conduct Authority 2013a). Some have, however, argued that the penalties imposed by UK regulators are meagre compared to other jurisdictions such as the US (Woods 2012).

The FSA was subsequently dissolved and its responsibilities regarding money laundering were taken over by the FCA, which has, as one of its objectives, to *"protect and enhance the integrity of the UK financial system"* (Financial Conduct Authority 2013a p. 6). Like the FSA, it supervises firms that are subject to the Money Laundering Regulation 2007, and it derives the same powers as the FSA under the FSMA Act 2000 and MLR 2007 (Financial Conduct Authority 2013a).

Money Laundering Regulations 2007

The MLR 2007 replaces the Money Laundering Regulation of 1993, 2001 and 2003 and has as one of its main purposes to ensure that regulated entities have systems and controls in place to prevent the use of financial system for money laundering and terrorist financing (H. M. Treasury 2007). It was introduced to implement the 2005 EU Directive that was issued as a result of the review of the 40 Recommendations of the FATF (Mitsilegas & Gilmore 2007). The main change to the previous regulation that it brought about was the introduction of the risk based approach to AML.

The Risk-Based Approach

The risk-based approach to AML is a concept that runs through all the recent regulations on AML. The concept is defined by the FATF as an approach that *"encompasses recognising the existence of the risk(s), undertaking an assessment of the risk(s) and developing strategies to manage and mitigate the identified risks"* (FATF 2007b p. 2). As a result of the various international obligations, the UK, through the MLR 2007, provides specific requirements for regulated entities to adopt the approach when conducting due diligence, monitoring customers' transactions and establishing and maintaining policies and procedures. The UK is, therefore, operating the approach as confirmed by the FATF in its assessment of the UK AML regime (FATF 2007c) and the FCA in its document on the approach to regulation (Financial Services Authority 2011). Although the risk-based approach is a step forward compared with the rule-based approach (de Koker 2009; de Wit 2007; van den Broek

2011), there are still some *"intrinsic (and very real) difficulties in handling the relationship between risk and AML"* (Demetis & Angell 2007 p. 424).

Some of these difficulties stemmed from the concept of risk itself, and its application in AML. Risk is a difficult concept to define (Haimes 2009). The term has been defined differently by different scholars from different disciplines. Some have defined it in terms of probability and impact (Guerron-Quintana 2012), while others have defined it in terms of hazard (Arvai 2007). Similarly, others have distinguished pure risk from speculative risk with the former being the situation where there is no chance of gain while in the latter there is a chance for gain (Williams 1966). There are also different perceptions of risk between experts and the public, according to Gibbs, Gore, McGarrell and Rivers (2010). Without a clear definition of the term, even in legislations (Ross & Hannan 2007), it may be used in one way and understood in another way.

Another source of difficulty is the lack of distinction between risk and uncertainty. Although the approach is called a risk-based approach, the situation in AML may be more akin to the situation of uncertainty because of the dominant role that uncertainty plays in AML environment.

There may also be the different understanding of the approach within the AML environment. What the regulators understand as a risk-based approach may not necessarily be the same understanding of the regulated. A regulated entity may, for example, implement what it believes is a risk based approach only to be told that by the regulators that their approach is not the right approach to follow.

National Crime Agency/Serious Organised Crime Agency

The role of FCA is complemented by Serious Organised Crime Agency (SOCA) which, until recently, was the designated financial intelligence unit (FIU) in the UK that was responsible for collecting suspicious activity reports from the regulated entities for analysis and investigation (Sproat 2007). The function and powers of SOCA was, however, taken over by National Crime Agency (NCA), an agency that commenced operation in 2013 (National Crime Agency 2013a).

SOCA came into existence as a result of the Serious Organised Crime and Police Act of 2005. The main purpose of the agency was to deal with the threat of organised crime. It took over the functions of the National Crime Squad (NCS) and the National Criminal Intelligence Service (NCIS), which was the UK Financial Intelligence Unit (UKFIU), the role of HRMC connected with drug trafficking and related financial crimes and immigration services related to organised immigration (Ryder 2008). It derived its powers from the Proceeds of Crime Act 2002 (Sproat 2007).

Proceeds of Crime Act 2002

The Proceeds of Crime Act was enacted in 2002 to establish the asset recovery agency, make provision for confiscation orders, allow for the recovery of criminal properties, make provision about money laundering, investigation and oversees cooperation (Proceeds of Crime Act 2002).

It specifically criminalised money laundering and conspiracy to commit a money laundering offence through the provisions of s. 327, 328 and 329, and imposed a maximum penalty of 14 years for breach of the principal offences mentioned in the three sections.

The first principal offence involves concealing, disguising converting transferring and recovering of criminal property from the UK (s. 327). The second concerns assisting a person to retain a criminal property (s. 328). The obligations of banks in this regard are, therefore, to immediately disclose information about which they are suspicious to NCA as soon as they become aware of it. The third offence relates to the acquisition, use or possession of criminal property as define in the law (s. 329).

In summary, the UK *"has a comprehensive legal structure to combat money laundering and terrorist financing"* (FATF 2007c p. 4), but at the heart of it is what some consider as imposing *"extensive and onerous reporting obligation"* (Marshall 2004 p. 111) as a resulted of the expansion of predicate offences and widening the scope of regulated entities. Like other jurisdiction, the UK also imposed the responsibility of preventing money laundering on the regulated entities, the *"unofficial policemen"* (Marshall 2004 p. 111) for combating money laundering. The UK regulatory environment also places high priority on asset recovery, the proceeds of which is normally divided between the treasury, prosecuting agencies, police and courts on the following basis: *"Treasury receives 1/2, Police 1/6, Prosecuting Authority (e.g. CPS) 1/6, Court Service 1/6"* (Masters 2008 p. 117).

The Role of a Money Laundering Reporting Officer (MLRO)

Role of an MLRO

The role of an MLRO was first introduced to UK regulation in 1994 (Bosworth-Davies 1998) following the enactment of the Money Laundering Regulation 1993. The act requires a firm to identify an *"appropriate person"* to receive internal reports on suspicious money laundering activities described in section 327: 329 of POCA 2002, evaluate the reports in the light of other relevant information and report it to law enforcement when the conditions of reporting are met. The term was subsequently changed from *"appropriate person"* to a *"nominated officer"* in s. 330 of POCA 2002 and the MLR 2003 in s. 7. Although the laws did not specifically mention money laundering reporting officer but in practice, and based on the FSA (now FCA) guidance in SYSC 3.2.6, a money laundering reporting officer is the designated nominated officer that is responsible for external reporting of suspicious activities (FATF 2007c; Financial Conduct Authority 2013b).

The requirement to appoint an MLRO (or a nominated officer) is not restricted to the regulated sector alone as firms outside the regulated sector may also appoint a nominated officer to serve in the same capacity (CPS 2010). A sole trader may not, however, appoint an MLRO because of his status as a single individual, but he serves as the nominated officer responsible for the reporting responsibilities (National Crime Agency 2014). This may highlight one of the reasons for having the difference between an MLRO and a nominated officer; another reason relates to the role of a deputy money laundering reporting officer in regulated entities.

A deputy money laundering reporting officer can also act as a nominated officer once that responsibility is assigned to him by the organisation (JMLSG 2011). This practice is common because of the size and complexity of some banks, and the workload of MLROs (Webb 2004). One MLRO may not be able to perform all the duties of a nominated officer given the various units in banks such as retail, investment and private banking units. This is evidence from the case of 2012) where the MLRO assigned the role of a nominated officer to a staff member in the private banking arm of the group, and it was held that the assignee was competent to act as a nominated office for the purpose of POCA 2002. In this case, therefore, both the MLRO and the deputy can receive and give consent for a prohibited act to be performed in addition to other reporting responsibilities. The prohibited acts are activities in violation of s. 327, 328 and 329 of POCA 2002 discussed in Section "The UK Regulatory Environment".

The role of an MLRO is, however, not restricted to the reporting responsibility. Most MLROs combine their role with other functions (Webb 2004). An MLRO department can also reside in other departments in a bank, but the most common area is the compliance department (Bosworth-Davies 1998; Webb 2004).

Main Duties of an MLRO

The main duties of an MLRO are to receive internal report about money laundering activities from within an organisation and the report it to law enforcement. Employees in the organisation are, therefore, required to report suspicious activities to the MLROs. He will then review and evaluate them based on the internal report, other available information and using his skill and experience, determine if they are suspicious after which he will report them to law enforcement (Proceeds of Crime Act 2002). MLROs are, therefore, essentially liaison officers between banks and regulators in the implementation of the provisions of various anti-money laundering regulations. Their role is however risky because they can go to jail for up to five years if they fail to fulfil their primary responsibility of reporting suspicious activities (s. 334 (2)). Furthermore,

Section 20 of the Money laundering Regulation 2007 also provides requirements for establishing and maintaining policies and procedures to prevent money laundering and terrorist financing activities.

Reporting Suspicious Activities

Under s. 338 of the Proceeds of Crime Acts (2002), there are at least three ways of making a report; reporting before a suspicious activity is committed, report while the activity is being committed and reporting after the reported activity has been committed. Once an MLRO is aware that an activity is suspicious, he is obliged to report the activity; failure to do so is an offence that is punishable under the law. There may, however, be a situation where the knowledge came to him while the activity is being committed. In this situation, he is also obliged to report as soon as he becomes aware that the activities are suspicious. In other instances, an MLRO will only become aware of the activity as suspicious after the activity must have been completed. In this instance, he is required to report the activity as soon as he becomes aware of it.

In the first two instances, when an MLRO becomes aware of the transaction as suspicious, he is not allowed to give consent for the transaction to be completed without the express consent of a competent authority, in this case the UK Financial Intelligence Unit, which is now part of the NCA (National Crime Agency 2013c). If, however, he gives consent without the approval of the UKFIU, he has committed a money laundering office under section 334 of PoCA 2002.

An MLRO can, however, give consent once he has received approval from the UKFIU. The process of obtaining consent starts with filing a normal suspicious activity report, usually online, and specifying, in the form, that he is requesting for a consent to perform a prohibited act. The UKFIU would then assess his request and either approve or reject it. If within seven working days of submitting the request, he did not receive a response from the authorities, he can give consent for the transaction to be completed, and would not be liable for breach of the reporting requirement. Even if consent is refused within the seven days, an MLRO can still continue with the transaction after 31 calendar days of the refusal if no further action is taken by the authorities. This process is highlighted in National Crime Agency (2013b), the guidance note produced by the UKFIU to share perspectives on the suspicious activity reporting regime (National Crime Agency 2013c).

While the report is being assessed by the UKFIU, an MLRO or any other individual for that matter is not allowed to disclose the issue to the customer whose activity is being reported. Any person who discloses any information that may jeopardise an investigation has committed the offence of tipping off, which has the same penalty as failure to disclose a suspicious activity. An MLRO is, however, immune from civil or criminal liability as regard his obligation under the contract with the customer as provided in section 337 (1) of the Act.

Other Duties

In addition to evaluating internal reports and sending them to law enforcement, an MLRO, as the head of the MLRO specialised unit (Canhoto 2008), is also responsible for ensuring that his organisation is complying with anti-money laundering laws as stated in SYSC 3.2.6 (Financial Conduct Authority 2013b). To ensure compliance, an MLRO has at least two sources of guidance to assist him; the guidance from the JMLSG and the FCA. The FCA guidance is contained in its handbook (Financial Conduct Authority 2013b) while the guidance from the JMLSG is contain in its approved guidance (JMLSG 2011).

Further details of MLRO obligations are contained in the JMLSG (2011) report which also includes responsibility for evaluating products and services to ensure that they are free from money laundering risk as well as advising senior management on changes to regulations and the intentions of regulators regarding money laundering. Part of his responsibility to senior management also includes preparing an annual report about the adequacy of systems and controls to prevent the use of the firm's system for money laundering (JMLSG 2011).

Furthermore, a money laundering reporting officer is also usually responsible for developing and implementing policies and procedures relating to AML, ensuring that they are communicated to all staff.

An MLRO is also responsible for making sure that employees are trained first to identify suspicious activities and secondly are aware of the provision of various laws and regulation affecting them. To achieve this purpose, he develops training material; update them regularly to capture evolving threats and changes in regulations. He may also involve external consultants to deliver the training while maintaining the responsibility for the delivery and effectiveness of the training. Training can be done in-house, outside the organisation, face to face, online-line or combination of approaches. The aim is to ensure that employees are adequately trained to respond to the threat of money laundering that they may come across while performing their duties (JMLSG 2011). Failure to comply with these and other AML requirements can lead to penalties on both banks and MLROs as seen in the case of FSA and Habib Bank AG Zurich (Financial Service Authority 2012b).

Qualification

It is also a requirement for a firm to ensure that an MLRO has the requisite authority, skill, qualification and independence to enable him perform his duties. (Financial Conduct Authority 2013b; JMLSG 2011). He should also be availed of the necessary resources that would allow him to perform his duties effectively (JMLSG 2011). These provisions, according to a participant in the study, were as a result of the practice in the early days of AML where some banks used to appoint junior staff as their MLROs. An example of this practice, he stated, was a bank that appointed a 19-year-old clerk as their MLRO.

Conclusion

Money laundering has been in existence for centuries, but it was only in the past few decades that real efforts were made to tackle it. The United Nation was the first international body that started the anti-money laundering effort before the FATF was formed specifically to deal with it.

The approach for dealing with AML was initialled the ruled-based approach, but the risk based approach was adopted to ensure that resources utilised are commensurate with the risk identified.

The UK has been at the forefront of the fight against money laundering, being an active member of the FATF among other international efforts. The UK is also one of the biggest financial centres in the world accounting for huge money laundering activities through its financial system. It has implemented various recommendations for dealing with money laundering and has enacted laws and regulations to ensure that its financial system is not used for money laundering. The effectiveness of its approach is, however, doubtful.

To understand the UK anti-money laundering environment, the research underpinning this book focused on getting the perspective of MLROs whose duty essentially is to receive reports of suspicious money laundering activities within their banks and report them to law enforcement for the purpose of detecting and preventing money laundering activities.

In this chapter, the history of AML was briefly described and narrowing the discussing to the UK regulatory environment. The role and responsibility of an MLRO were also highlighted to provide a context for the discussion that will come later. The chapter is, therefore, not a critical review of the literature, but it is presented to provide a context for the next chapter on the self-protecting theory. In that chapter, the theory will be presented and, in the process, the role of an MLRO and the impact of various regulations will be discussed.

3

Self-Protecting Theory – A Theory of MLROs

The assumption of the reader, he should be advised, is that all concepts are grounded and that the massive grounding effort could not be shown in writing.

(Glaser 1978 p. 134)

Introduction

This chapter presents the *self-protecting theory*, which explains how MLROs are dealing with their main concern of *unfair pressure*. It may be recalled that grounded theory is about finding the concerns of participants and discovering a theory that explains that main concern (Glaser 1978; Glaser 2001). Accordingly, the main questions, as introduced in Chap. 1, are:

What are the concerns of MLROs? and how are they resolving them?

In the following section, the main concern of *unfair pressure* discovered in the research will be discussed and then the *protecting* behaviour for resolving it will follow. Before then, however, a section will be

A.U. Bello, *Improving Anti-Money Laundering Compliance*,
Palgrave Studies in Risk, Crime and Society,
DOI 10.1007/978-3-319-43264-9_3

presented explaining the major entities, as discovered in the study, related to the theory (banks, regulators and MLROs) to provide context for understanding the process of conceptualisation leading to the discovery of the theory. A section is then included that shows the details of how the theory emerged from a process of integration using the theoretical code introduced in Chap. 1. At the end, the self-protecting framework discovered from the theory will be discussed to show the potential contribution of the theory. A detailed discussion on the contribution will, however, be presented in Chap. 6.

In line with classical grounded theory, each concept was discovered through a rigorous process of conceptualisation and constant comparison as summarised below. The aim of this summary is, therefore, to show that all concepts discussed in this chapter are grounded since the "*massive grounding effort could not be shown in writing*" (Glaser 1978 p. 134). Each concept will, however, be illustrated and referenced using footnotes, with at least one quotation from field notes, reference to previous chapters, and reference to theoretical memos. These illustrations are representative, as such, they are not the only sources of evidence for the concepts presented. This is because each concept is a combination of many incidents, analysed in several memos and sorted with several other concepts. To make the chapter more comprehensible, main concepts will be shown in italics and excerpts from data will be included in a box and in italics.

Overview of the Self-protecting Theory

This study is about *self- protecting*, a theory suggesting that *unfair pressure* makes compliance officers do whatever they can to protect themselves rather than do what they are expected to do. This book is, however, about how MLROs are *discharging* their responsibility to protect themselves rather than *complying* with regulation to prevent money laundering.

The main concern of MLROs is the *unfair pressure* placed on them by *banks* on the one hand, and *regulators* on the other. *Banks* are usually more concerned with returns to shareholders while *regulators* are more concerned with preventing money laundering. They, however, have a stake in each other's interest, because banks are also concerned with the impact of money laundering on their profitability and regulators are also concerned about the soundness of the banking system. It is this conflicting pressure most of which is perceived by MLROs to be unfair that is the main source of their concern. It is worth noting that this conflicting interest between banks and regulators is the key to understanding the *self-protecting* theory. This came out forcefully from the data with almost all participants highlighting it. One participant even said:

> "In as far I am concerned, banks are only concerned with preventing fraud but not money laundering. Fraud affects the profitability of the bank, but in the case of money laundering it may even affect profitability negatively". *He added that* "Ok, there is the moral issue, but apart from that it doesn't make sense to prevent customers from bringing deposits that will increase the bank's profitability".

The main sources of *unfair pressure* are regulatory and organisational concerns. Regulatory concerns are mainly related to *unfair pressure* from regulators through *defective regulation, naïve regulators, damage to reputation* and *shifting expectation*. Organisational concerns, on the other hand, relate mainly to *unfair pressure* from banks through *lack of resources* and *marginal management* – a concept that deals with the difficulty of getting the required support from other employees within the bank because they are not directly under the control of an MLRO. MLROs betray their thoughts on what is unfair and from which direction it is coming from through their constant *complaining* about the contradiction of the job and its pressure. When most of the complaint is against a bank, for example, then the *unfair pressure* is coming from the bank, but when it is against regulators then *unfair pressure* is coming from the regulators.

To resolve their problems, MLROs adopt a variety of strategies, but the core category that resolves their main concern of *unfair pressure* is the *protecting* category. *Protecting,* is concerned with *protecting* oneself from *unfair pressure* instead of conforming to the requirement of the role. *Discharging* and *communicating* are the main methods of *self-protecting*. *Discharging* to protect is done through *assessing* to protect, *reporting* to protect, *learning* to protect and *automating* to protect; rather than *assessing* to prevent, *reporting* to prevent, *learning* to prevent and *automating* to prevent. *Communicating*, on the other hand, is done through *dialogue, justifying* and *threat*.

There is, however, a concept called *aligning* that indicates the allegiance of an MLRO. The concept, which has two properties called *interest* and *belief*, indicates whether an MLRO is mostly *discharging* or *communicating*. If an MLRO's interest is aligned with that of the bank, for example, and he believes the pressure from the regulators is unfair, then he is *discharging* to protect himself against regulators. If, however, his interest aligns with the interests of regulators and he believes that the pressure from the bank is unfair, then he is *communicating* to protect himself against the bank. As will be seen later, what is predominantly happening within the UK banking sector is that MLROs are more aligned with banks and, therefore, *discharging* to protect than they are aligned with regulators, though *communicating* to protect is also not far behind since both methods are used to deal with *unfair pressure*.

In essence, by *aligning* with one party, an MLRO is effectively *protecting* himself against the other and vice versa. Even though the findings in the research show that MLROs are mainly *aligning* themselves with banks and *protecting* themselves against regulators, the theory also explains what happens in a situation where they are *aligning* with regulators and *protecting* themselves against the banks and even where there is fair pressure from both parties. These situations are depicted in a framework discovered in the research to assist in evaluating AML compliance as detailed later in this chapter.

Related Entities

The description of the entities are as found in the study and not necessarily the understanding of the terms in the literature and practice, though differences in definition, if any, are insignificant.

Regulators

There are two main types of AML regulators; *financial regulators* that regulate the banking industry as a whole and *law enforcement agencies* that deal with the investigation and prosecution of money laundering.

Financial regulators usually deal with banks to a greater extent than *law enforcement agencies*. This is because *financial regulators* are not only concerned with making sure that banks comply with money laundering regulations, they are also concerned with ensuring the soundness of the banking industry. *Law enforcement agencies*, on the other hand, are not only dealing with money laundering, but they are also dealing with other crimes involving fraud, terrorism and tax issues among others. Even though money laundering is a criminal offence and MLROs are supposed to report suspicious activities to law enforcement, banks in the UK are more involved with financial regulators than with law enforcement agencies.

Banks

There are also different types of banks. There are *big* and *small* sized banks: size being measured in terms of volume of transactions, value of transactions, number of customers or number of locations. A commercial bank, for example, is traditionally associated with having more transactions, but not necessarily transactions of high value. They also tend to have more customers and more branches. Investment banks, on the other hand, have fewer transactions, but most of the transactions are of high value. They also tend to have fewer customers and a minimal branch network in contrast to commercial banks. Even within commercial banking, there are other divisions like retail banking, private banking and building societies. While retail banking is usually bigger, a private bank is smaller in term of its customer base and number of transactions. A building society can be large, but it usually localised to one geographical location.

Mlro

MLROs are liaison officers between banks and regulators. They sit in the middle, but are employees of banks. Their role, the nature and severity of pressure they face depends on the type of the financial institutions they work for and the kind of regulators that they are dealing with. Their roles can be solely to deal with AML compliance or they can combine it with other compliance activities. Some are nominated officers; employees that are registered with regulators to perform MLRO functions, while others are not registered but nevertheless perform the same function as MLROs and are called deputy MLROs.

MLROs are usually highly *experienced* and *capable* because of the requirement of regulation to appoint an MLRO with sufficient authority. Some are *hands-on* MLROs while others are *hands-off* depending on the financial institution and its size. However defined, they are usually *stressed* because of *unfair pressure, lonely* and *independent* because of dealing with conflicting interest. Most are *underappreciated* since it is difficult to serve two masters at the same time, and some are *tolerated* for their job is usually not considered essential. In addition, they are also *overworked* because of *under resources*; they are made *scapegoats* because of their role as nominated officers, and they are mostly *willing* because of their background in law enforcement and compliance. They can, however, be *self-interested* in order to survive the stress and the conflicting pressure from banks and regulators.

Unfair Pressure as the Main Concern

One of the defining differences between classical grounded theory and other qualitative methodologies is that a research problem, in classical grounded theory, is derived from data through interview of participants, for example, while in some other methodologies the research problem is derived from the literature (Jones & Noble 2007). *Unfair pressure* was discovered during the research as the main concern of MLROs. It is, therefore, the research problem.

It is important to start by explaining why unfair is a qualifying pressure. The full import of this would become clear as the theory is explained, but suffice to say that it is not only pressure that concerns MLROs. Pressure, therefore, has two dimensions: fair and unfair, and it is the *unfair pressure* that is the source of concern which MLROs are continually resolving. There are two primary sources of *unfair pressure* for MLROs. The major source is *regulatory concern*, and the other is *organisational concern*.

Although most of the pressure is directly from regulators (regulatory concerns) and banks (organisational concerns), there are some *indirect pressures* that are transferred to MLROs through the bank by customers, lawyers, consultants, auditors, for example, and through the regulators from international bodies like the FATF, public and politicians. As more pressure is exerted on banks and regulators this is transferred to MLROs

Regulatory Concern as a Source of Unfair Pressure

Regulatory concerns are concerns expressed by MLROs that are coming from the side of the regulators. They are *defective regulation, naïve regulators, damage to reputation* and *shifting expectation.*

Defective Regulation

The concept of *defective regulations* was generated during coding and memoing of the first field note as *faulty regulation* but was changed to *defective regulation* later during analysis. The following statement of one participant illustrates the first time that the code was generated. In the first interview, the participant narrated a story about an MLRO that was being prosecuted for reporting a suspicious activity but because of intense pressure from the customer whose transaction was reported, he had to allow the transaction to be completed before getting a response from the authorities. *"An honest man he is" he stated, "but luckily the prosecutors had to drop the case. Why? Because it is not in the public interest to prosecute him. This is a man that reported a case that others failed the report!".*

Defective regulation has three main properties, namely; *suspicious activity reporting, watch list* and the *risk-based approach.*

Suspicious Activity Reporting (SAR)

It is almost unanimous that the consent regime of SAR regulation is not fit for purpose and is bordering on unworkable. "*The consent regime is rubbish*" was one of the quotes from an MLRO. For a suspicious transaction that is not completed, an MLRO is supposed to obtain consent from regulators first before completing the transaction. During the "*limbo*" period when they had to wait for consent, but before they complete the transaction, some MLROs go under intense and excruciating pressure. They give excuses to customers on why they cannot execute their request. *"Our system is down"* is no more a valid reason for delaying a transaction. According to one MLRO "*some would say that they have a problem with their system, but if customers call head office, they will be told that the system is working*". Some MLROs, because of the sustained pressure from customers, have to compromise their position by informing customers about the reason for the delay. This is, however, a tipping-off offence that can lead to an MLRO being prosecuted for breaching AML regulations (section "The UK Regulatory Environment"). For those that stood their ground, the pressure is so much that it is almost unbearable. One of them, an MLRO of a small bank, decided to shut down the operation of a whole branch to avoid the constant and consistent pressure from a customer whose transaction was delayed.

As a result of this pressure, MLROs consider it unfair to place them in a position where they are compelled to lie or commit a tipping-off offence. The tipping-off provision is *"rubbish"*, according to that participant, because the regulation on tipping-off is in the public domain and sometimes obtaining consent is seen as a mere formality as consent is given even though it is clear to the MLRO that the transaction is suspicious. Moreover, a perceptive customer would be able to conclude that the reason his transaction is suspended is because of a money laundering inquiry. The courts, in the case of Shah vs HSBC Private Bank (UK) Limited [2012] EWHC 1283, even recognised that Shah must have known that he is under enquiry. It is, therefore, considered unfair to oblige MLROs to keep the information from customers and be subjected to pressure which may lead to civil action against them. According to one participant, "the *pressure is too much, that is why my blood pressure is high. But I would rather face a civil case than go to prison*". The pressure from customers is, however, mainly a concern for small banks because big banks can shield their MLROs by creating a barrier between them such that there is no direct contact between customers and MLROs.

Some MLROs also consider it unfair to protect themselves at the expense of customers and banks, but they are left with no option because of their *interest* since *"at the end of the day you are in it for the money"*, according to the first MLRO that was interviewed. Customers may lose their businesses if they are not allowed to execute their transactions because of the consent requirement; banks may also lose customers whose transactions are delayed. In addition, there may be indirect losses to MLROs whose salaries depend on the profitability of the banks. All this is because of the consent requirement that places unnecessary pressure on MLROs. According to one MLRO, for example,

> With consent, you sent a request to SOCA, wait for several days for a response which can take up to 30 days and you are not supposed to tell customers. What do you do? We sometimes tell them that there is a problem with our system or the documentation or something of that nature. We say all these even though we are not supposed to lie.

It is not only the consent regime that is considered unfair. Lack of feedback on suspicious activity reports is also a concern to MLROs. A situation where an MLRO would report an activity but would receive no feedback from regulators on whether the SAR has led to a successful prosecution or not is also considered unfair.

Watch Lists

Watch list is another source of concern to MLROs because of the number of lists and inconsistency contain in them. The two lists that are of a great concern to MLROs are the sanction and Politically Exposed Persons (PEP) lists that contain names of persons linked to terrorism and public figures respectively.

There are so many lists to deal with including lists from the United States (US), the European Union (EU), United Nations (UN) and many other jurisdictions and organisations. Dealing with these lists is *"an administrative nightmare"* said one MLRO. Not only are the lists many, but they also overlap and contain inconsistencies and duplications. This concern is, however, more pronounced for MLROs of international banks that are dealing with multiple jurisdictions and especially those that are operating in the US that are strict in implementing regulations over sanction. The concern is, however, not restricted to

MLROs of international banks because local banks in the UK also have to deal with other lists from the EU, for example.

Hence, the main issue for MLROs is the difficulty in matching customers against unstructured lists of named individuals on the *watch lists*. This is because the order of names, spelling and the identifying details can be so confusing and inconsistent. "*It is a boring job*" said one MLRO and *"a labour intensive work with lots of false positives"* said another. An MLRO may also know that they do not have a particular name in their database based on his own risk assessment, but is nevertheless required to comply with the regulation and in the process expending limited resources in time, effort and money. This is particular true for local banks with limited international operation. Requiring them to check against names that are, in all likelihood, not going to exist in their database is unfair, given the concern over resources. *"We have been using the system for some time now, but we have not identified any of our customers on the sanction list so far"* is the response of one MLRO who consider it unfair to spend huge resources when it is unlikely that they have customers on the lists.

The same problem of duplication and lack of structure also applies to PEP list. In addition, the list is potentially endless because a bank must ensure that it is screening customers against the list of PEPs in at least all the high-risk countries (section "History of Anti-Money Laundering"). This, coupled with the fact that the list, by its nature, is constantly changing because the number of people on the list goes beyond recognised high profile individuals, but also their immediate family and close associates. On dealing with PEP list, one MLRO said in frustration, that they want to help regulators,"*but with information and intelligence, not by chasing papers*".

In summary, what is unfair about the *watch list* is its lack of structure and lack of consistency. Despite these concerns, an MLRO is required to comply with the *watch list* regulations, whether he believes in it or not. What makes the *watch list* even more unfair for some MLROs is their belief that it is a tool to achieve political objectives rather than a genuine effort to prevent money laundering and terrorism.

Risk-based Approach

The *risk-based approach* is also another manifestation of *defective regulation*. The complaint mainly revolves around the difficulty in implementing it because the spirit of the approach is not adhered to. An MLRO may decide that a transaction is not suspicious, based on his own assessment, but he would be blamed by regulators for not identifying it as suspicious, based on the assessment of regulators. It is this ownership of assessment that is considered unfair by MLROs. Another element is that the volume of transactions is huge; as such, MLROs may not be able to identify most suspicious activities because of the *under resources* concern mentioned earlier.

Some MLROs believe it is unfair for regulators to require banks to follow the *risk-based approach* and then issue guidelines on assessment that undermines the approach. Although they are called guides, MRLOs inherently know that they are expected to follow them, the failure of which may cost them dearly (section "The UK Regulatory Environment"). It is not surprising that many MLROs consider the *risk-based approach* a theory that has little bearing in practice, mainly because of the prescriptive nature of regulatory expectation.

The *risk-based approach* can, however, be viewed from two perspectives. Small MLRO functions dealing with fewer transactions like private banking units may prefer the *risk-based approach* because it is easy to implement, but for MLROs functioning in big retail banks that deal with a huge volume of transactions, the *risk-based approach* is not appropriate. They would rather employ technology to support their assessment, despite its limitation. The limitation relates to the use of a standard set of rules that may not be applicable to every situation.

Shifting Expectation

The second regulatory concern is *shifting expectation*, which is mainly related to the explicit and implicit expectation of regulators. Regulators are constantly issuing new guidelines, enacting and amending laws and regulations, changing policies and procedures. It is this speed and amount of regulation that they consider unfair. One MLRO was complaining that a front officer will be instructed to do a job in a certain way today, but before he could even have a chance to do it, he will be told to do it in another way tomorrow because of new rules and regulations. The concern is that regulators do not consider the logistics and impact of changing regulation, but they require immediate implementation, and this is unfair. Moreover, it is unfair to the front officers who have to deal with constant changes in regulation; unfair on banks because of the increased cost of regulation and unfair on MLROs who have to ensure compliance.

Shifting expectation is not necessarily constrained to rules and regulations. Regulators sometimes implicitly expect MLROs to do their job in a certain way, which may not even be required by regulations. The case of the *risk-based approach* is an example of the relationship between the requirement of the law and expectation of regulators. An MLRO is not certain that his interpretation of the law meets the regulators' expectation. As regards reporting suspicious activities, for example, there is the expectation that the size of a bank determines the number of suspicious activity reports. Any big bank that submits less than expected is considered to be failing in its duties resulting in threat of enforcement action.

Damage to Reputation

MRLOs are also concerned about damage to their reputation. The sources of this concern are mainly the *fear* of prosecution, *fear* of civil liability and *fear* of being named and shamed on the pages of Newspapers. Although MLROs agree that it is fair to punish them for deliberate breach of regulations, dereliction of duty and conspiracy, they believe it is unfair to punish them for honest error in judgment when *assessing* a transaction, *use of discretion* because for *lack of resources* and errors and mistakes that are not deliberate and careless. This concern was captured by one MLRO who said *"this is not fair. I am an honest individual. I don't even have a parking ticket, but I can go to jail for acts committed by another person"*. Another MLRO was even more uncharitable, *"it is a draconian process"*, he concluded.

It is this obsession with enforcing systems and controls and increased rhetoric of enforcement rather than pursuing money launderers that are the sources of *unfair pressure* on MLROs. MLROs have this perception of prosecution ingrained in their minds. They believe it is unfair to prosecute and penalise MLROs because of the lasting impact it has on their reputation and image. Prosecuting and penalising MLROs may lead to the break-up of family relationship, a particular concern of one MLRO who said; *"what would I tell my family?"* They may also lose their jobs and be the object of scorn in the society for matters beyond their control. This is made worse when they see money launderers escaping justice because of *defective regulation*; receiving light sentences because of the poor sentencing regime, and enjoying their ill-gotten wealth because of the difficulty in prosecuting money laundering offences.

Naive Regulators

The last property of regulatory concern is *naive regulators*. The concern relates to some regulator's *lack of understanding* of banking operations and *inexperience* and the *lack of skill* of some enforcement officers. Investment banking, for example, is different from retail banking; *lack of understanding* of this difference makes regulators issue blanket regulation that might suit one but not the other. A situation where fresh graduates are sent to banks without the necessary skills to perform their duties is a great source of concern to MLROs and is considered unfair. Even when matured officers are sent to banks, they often lack the experience because of high staff turnover. According to one MLRO, enforcing regulations are conducted by people that do not understand financial crimes and money laundering. He stated *"[name of authority] doesn't understand what we are going through. Some of their employees are not experienced, partly because there is a lot of staff turnover in the organisation"*.

There is also the concern that regulators do not have enough resources to regulate AML in the banking sector. A situation where there are only 20 specialists dealing with 29,000 firms is not only unfeasible but also naive. So also is the expectation that MLROs will give their best to regulators because of potential punishment when it is banks that give immediate reward.

In summary, the main points that have emerged are *defective regulation, shifting expectation, damage to reputation* and *naïve regulators.*

Organisational Concern as a Source of Unfair Pressure

The other source of *unfair pressure* comes from the side of banks. The two primary sources of *unfair pressure* are *under resources* and *marginal management.*

Under Resources

The main source of *unfair pressure* under organisational concern is lack of resources. *Under resources* fall into three main types: *lack of financial resources, lack of time* and *lack of human resources.*

The first concern is lack of funds to finance the operations of an MLRO function. The foremost concern, in this category, is finding money to purchase software that would automate *assessing* and *reporting* functions. Since MLROs are well aware that they do not have enough human resources and time to do their work, the easiest way to solve the problem is to have technology that would enable them fulfil their responsibilities. To the extent that they lack the resources constitutes a great source of concern. Some are also concerned about the level of salary paid to MLROs. Even though the salary of an MLRO may rank higher than that the salary of a person holding a similar position within the organisation, some believe the risks involved are by far greater than the reward they are receiving. Examples of some of the risks include the risk of prosecution, civil litigation and damage to reputation. The concept of *punishment* that covers these risks was first generated during the memoing and it has been consistently appearing throughout.

The other concern is *the lack of time* mainly due to MLROs' other compliance activities. This, however, depends on the size of the bank. Small banks usually have MLROs that are also compliance officers, while bigger banks are more likely to have MLROs that only focus on AML issues. Consequently, an MLRO with other roles would be more time constrained than another MLRO without other roles. This is sometimes offset by the nature of the bank: an MLRO of a big international bank would be more time constrained than an MLRO of a local bank even if his only role is that of an MLRO, though most big banks resolve this problem by appointing deputy MLROs to perform the function. The range of products, number of transactions and number of supporting staff also determine whether time is a concern or not.

Finally, MLROs are also concerned about the lack of adequate employees to assist them in complying with AML regulations. Without a sufficient number of employees in an MLRO function, it is difficult for MLROs to perform their duties effectively. This is because of a large number of transactions, variety of products and services and locations of bank offices.

In conclusion, what most MLROs consider unfair relating to *lack of resources* is the reluctance by most banks to provide the required resources for the job. This is despite knowing that an MLRO cannot perform his duty properly without adequate resources. It is unfair to have to constantly justify the need for resources unlike managers in other departments that find it relatively easier to obtain funding. One participant who works in an MLRO department said *"surprisingly some compliance officers including MLROs want their banks to be penalised because that is the only way that will make the banks to take them seriously. Without any enforcement action, banks may not allocate enough resources to the department"*. One of the reasons for this unequal treatment is that MLROs function are viewed as "*cost centres*", with one MLRO admitting that "*my department cost the bank money; we do not bring money in. Ok I can save them money on fines and penalties, but how much is the penalty?*"

As a result of this, MLROs understand the reason why banks are reluctant to spend on an MLRO function, but they also understand the rationale for requiring banks to provide resources to prevent money laundering. This conflict increases pressure on MLROs making it difficult for them to convince banks to spend on technology, on the one hand, and convince regulators that a recommended control is unnecessary, on the other.

Marginal Management

Marginal management is a concept discovered to explain the difficulty faced by MLROs who need the support of employees that are not directly under their control. This lack of support from management, subordinates and colleagues who may not share the same interest with MLROs is a major organisational concern. Collectively, these employees are called marginal employees because MLROs have only marginal control over them.

This concern is evident when the role of an MLRO is considered (section "The Role of a Money Laundering Reporting Officer (MLRO)"). MLROs need front office staff to report unusual transactions they discover when dealing with customers; MLROs need relationship managers to disclose suspicious activities of their clients; and they also need IT managers to provide IT support for their operation. Take the example of the relationship between an IT manager and an MLRO. According to one MLRO, while an IT manager is concerned about the cost of purchasing a system for an MLRO function, an MLRO is concerned about the absence of a system that would enable him to do his job properly even if it is expensive. MLROs also need marketing managers to be conscious of AML issues when developing products and services. They need sales people, who some believe are *"more concerned with bonuses than preventing money laundering"*, to identify unusual activities. They also need the support of management to provide a compliance culture that is necessary for effective compliance.

The concern is, therefore, the inability of MLROs to receive the required level of support from marginal employees which they consider unfair given that an MLRO cannot function properly without the support of employees. One reason for the lack of support is because marginalemployees, rightly or wrongly, do not consider an MLRO function a strategic business unit. For a relationship and marketing officers that are profit oriented, for example, an MLRO function is unnecessary clog in the path to achieving bonus targets, though the attitude is slightly changing because of the increased spotlight on AML issues. Management attitude is also shifting because they are now more accountable for AML compliance.

Protecting as a Means of Resolving the Main Concern

The core category for dealing with unfair pressure is *protecting*. It is an in vivo idea derived from the data. *"It is all about self-preservation"* an MLRO emphasised when asked to discuss his role as an MLRO. *Protecting* is, therefore, a concept that encapsulates the idea of protecting oneself as an MLRO when performing one's duties while making sure that one is not exposed to risks of unfair pressure from regulators and banks.

There are two major means of protecting: *discharging* and *communicating*, which are used in dealing with *unfair pressure* from regulatory and organisational sources respectively. Because MLROs are under a lot of pressure from both the regulators, on one hand, and banks, on the other, *protecting* to them is the most logical course of action. There is, however, a category called *aligning*, a sub-core of *protecting*, that needs to be explained first in order to understand the core category. This is because *protecting* can be a response to *unfair pressure* from regulators when the MLRO is *aligning* with the bank or from the bank when the MLRO is *aligning* with regulators.

Aligning as a Sub-core of Self-protecting

MLROs are either aligned more with banks or aligned more with regulators because of conflicting interest between the two. We have earlier mentioned that banks are generally more concerned with returns to shareholders than with preventing money laundering. This is evident throughout the data and was captured by one MLRO, who said he would not blame regulators for putting pressure on bankers because that is the only way to ensure compliance since, according to him, there is no incentive for banks to prevent money laundering. *Interest* and *belief* are the two concepts that determine the alignment of MLROs.

Interest as a Property of Aligning

Interest has two main properties: *reward* and *punishment*. MLROs by definition are employees of banks, and as such, they have a certain level of loyalty to their banks; but they are also nominated officers, which make them directly responsible to regulators as regards AML compliance. Being employees of banks, they receive their *reward* mainly from banks in the form of salary, benefits among others, though they can also be rewarded by regulators through recognising their efforts at combating money laundering. An example of this, according to one participant, was when one MLRO "*detected a suspicious activity and reported it. Because of that they were able to burst the gang of criminals. He was given a congratulatory letter from the US SEC for his effort*".

Punishment, on the other hand, is mainly from regulators through prosecution, penalty, blacklisting and naming and shaming for not performing their responsibilities as expected. Banks can, however, punish MLROs by terminating their appointments or discriminating against them. In the main, however, banks *reward* and regulators *punish*.

The relationship between *reward* and *punishment* is interesting in that *reward* from banks is certain while *punishment* by regulators is uncertain. Left with these options, MLROs would rather align with banks because of the certainty of *reward* than align with regulators because of uncertainty of *punishment*. There is also a disparity between *reward* from banks and *punishment* from regulators, because the *punishment* is insignificant in relation to the *reward*. This is because although there is much talk about prosecuting banks for breach of AML regulations, in reality not much is happening. An MLRO was reminded of this when speaking to a business manager at a training session. The manager said that he has not seen bankers going to jail, so he was not concerned about the threat of prosecution. There are, however, cases of penalties and fine from financial regulators.

The question for MLROs is therefore: why trade certainty for uncertainty? Unless the punishment is higher than the *reward* and the likelihood of *punishment* is higher than for *reward*, MLROs would rather align with banks than align with regulators.

Belief as a Property of Aligning

The other property of *aligning* is *belief*. *Culture, conviction* and *ethics* are the three properties of *belief*. An MLRO that is convinced a piece of legislation is wrong, for example, would not be keen to implement it. Furthermore, a weak *culture* in the bank would discourage MLROs from following regulations. Their *ethics* may, however, override those concerns, and despite a weak *culture* in a bank and a lack of *belief* they may follow regulations because of their *upstanding*. The first concept under *belief* is *culture*, and the strong determinant of *culture* in an organisation is the "*tone at the top*". MLROs will more likely align with regulators if the *culture* in the organisation is good, but if the *culture* is weak with management more profit oriented at the expense of compliance, then it is more likely for them to align with banks unless their *ethics* is high. This is because the most important influence of alignment is the *interest* of an MLRO even more than his *belief*. And since the *interest* of most MLROs is served better by banks, they are more likely to align with banks than with regulators. The *culture* in a bank, which influences the culture of an MLRO, is, therefore, a very important and often repeated concept in the data with most MLROs emphasising its importance.

Conviction is the second concept of belief that determines alignment. If MLROs believe the purpose of money laundering is not for preventing money laundering but for political reasons, for example, or if they believe that regulations are defective, they would be reluctant to comply, but would rather discharge their responsibility to protect himself. If, however, MLROs believe in regulations, they would more likely align with regulators to prevent money laundering.

Finally, the ethical stances of MLROs determine with whom they align. Honest and upright MLROs would not conspire with their banks to facilitate money laundering. This trait may come from their background in law enforcement, a strong compliance culture or their personal ethical values. Their personal ethical values are what drove some of them to pursue a career as MLROs as stated by one participant who said he wanted to become a police officer, but settled for an MLRO because it is the closest to becoming one. A dishonest and corrupt MLRO may, however, conspire with the bank and customers to facilitate money laundering. *Conspiracy* in most cases is, however, a matter of *belief.* While an MLRO may breach money-laundering regulation believing that it is the right thing to do, regulators would, however, see it as *conspiring* to promote money laundering. There are instances of clear conspiracy, though, but this mostly involves the bank as a whole rather than individuals MLROs. This is evident in the two of the secondary data analysed when it was stated that

> "The nominated officer dismisses concerns escalated by staff without reasons being" *and* "He strategized with SCB's regulatory compliance staff by advising that "if SCB London were to ignore OFACs regulations AND SCB NY were not involved in any way & (2) had no knowledge of SCB Londons [sic] activities & (3) could not be said to be in a position to control SCB London, then IF OFAC discovered SCBLondons [sic] breach, there is nothing they could do against SCB London, or more importantly against SCBNY"".

This was further supported by a former MLRO who said "*So in essence, MLROs are not interested in preventing money laundering*".

In addition to being a property of *aligning*, belief, like *complaining*, is a strong indicator of unfairness. Whether a pressure is fair or unfair depends on the *belief* of an MLRO. If he believes that a regulation is unfair, then it is unfair even if regulators believe it is fair. There is also the relationship between *believe* and *interest.* It is more likely for an MLRO to *belief* in the fairness of a regulation or of a management decision if it aligns with his interest.

Having decided to align one way or the other an MLRO would protect himself using the ways of *protecting* mentioned earlier that is, *discharging* and *communicating.* This book now considers each of these categories in more detail.

Discharging as a Means of Protecting

Discharging is the primary way of dealing with *unfair pressure* resulting mainly from regulatory concern. There are five main categories of *discharging*: *assessing, reporting, learning, complaining* and *automating.*

Automating is, however, not as independent as the others because it is used mainly for *assessing* and *reporting*. It is, however, one of the most important tools for *discharging* and hence *self-protecting*.

Assessing as a Property of Discharging

Assessing is used mainly to resolve concerns relating to *defective regulations* and *damage to reputation*. It can also be used to resolve concerns over *shifting expectation* and *marginal management*. It has *balancing* and *using discretion* as its two major properties.

By *balancing*, an MLRO is constantly *assessing* whether to consider a transaction as suspicious or not based on the risk to himself, but not necessarily because of the risk of money laundering. One of the ways of *assessing* a transaction is using the *risk-based approach*, which is part of the requirement of UK regulation (section "The UK Regulatory Environment"). To some MLROs, however, the *risk-based approach* is only a tool for *discharging* their responsibilities to avoid *punishment* rather than *complying* to prevent money laundering. To most MLROs, therefore, especially those in big retail banks, the *risk-based approach* is just a theory because the *rule-based approach* is more practicable because of the defective nature of the *risk-based approach* mentioned earlier.

In *assessing* transactions, MLROs are constantly trying to find a balance between risk and reward, and then prioritise based on their *interest* after which they vigorous justify their decision for choosing one way or the other. In most cases, they align with banks and justify their decision, if need be, to the regulators. In instances when risk of punishment from the bank is low, MLROs would most likely assess a transaction that at best is unusual as suspicious instead of *assessing* it as a non-suspicious in order to avoid punishment from regulators for making an improper assessment. This *safe assessing*, a property of *balancing*, is contributing to the problem of excessive reporting because an MLRO has nothing to lose by making an inconsequential report to regulators. An example of striking a balance between risk and reward was highlighted by an encounter between a marketing department and an MLRO. According to the MLRO, the marketing department came up with an idea of a product, but when they were told that the product is not safe, they refused to listen. To protect himself from the bank in this type of situation, he sometimes has to accept the commercial reality that such products will be launched despite his reservations.

An MLRO also uses his *discretion* as a pragmatic way of dealing with *under resources* when *assessing* transactions. The use of *discretion* as a way of *assessing* is, however, problematic, because of the expectation of regulators. An MLRO may use his *discretion* because of the large number of transactions and lack of resources to deal with them, but on an enforcement visit, a regulator would fault his judgements without considering the circumstance under which he made those judgements. As a result of this, MLROs are now calling for the use of common sense in dealing with the problem of *under resourcing* and regulatory expectation. As one MLRO stated, when speaking about the use of technology, *"software is not the answer. Common sense and using the software correctly are better"*.

Assessing is not only used for *protecting*, but it can also be used to prevent money laundering. The difference between *assessing* to protect and *assessing* to prevent is subtle. The intention of an MLRO determines whether he is *assessing* to protect or he is *assessing* to prevent. Understanding the motivation of an MLRO is difficult, but by identifying his *interest* and belief, the intention of an MLRO can be discerned. The intention of an MLRO that aligns with the bank at the expense of regulators, for example, is *assessing* to protect, while the intention of an MLRO that aligns with regulators at the expense of the bank is *assessing* to prevent.

Reporting as a Way of Discharging

Reporting is also mainly used to resolve the concern over *defective regulation* concern, *damage to reputation* and *shifting expectation*. It has two categories; *playing safe* (safe reporting) and *defending*. MLROs having assessed a transaction are left with two choices; to report or not to report. If they decide to report, how and what are they going to report? And if they decide not to report, how are they going to defend their decisions?

Playing Safe as a Property of Reporting

As a result of their *balancing* activity, if they decide a transaction is low risk to their interest they will then report it to law enforcement to show that they are *discharging* their responsibilities. This is because of the expectation of regulators that banks that report suspicious activities are more compliant that those that do not. MLROs are aware of this expectation and are prepared to send more reports to satisfy regulators' expectations. This was highlighted by one MLRO who said they could play *"the numbers game"* if that is what the regulators want. By *playing safe* an MLRO is dealing with the *regulatory concerns* but in the process worsening the excessive reporting problem that exists in AML compliance (Goldby 2012; Marshall 2004). A clear example of *playing safe* is continuous reporting. An MLRO may be convinced that an activity is suspicious or even a money laundering activity, but having requested and obtained consent from regulators to allow the activity, he continues to report similar activities *"so as not to breach consent regulation"* instead of ending the relationship. His interest is to protect himself, and by continuous reporting, he is protecting himself from regulators as well as protecting himself from the bank, since he is complying with regulation as well as protecting the bank from losing a customer.

Defending as a Property of Reporting

The other property of *reporting* is *defending*. Having decided one way or the other, an MLRO would then have to defend his judgement. If he decides that an activity is suspicious, he then has to convince the bank that it is indeed suspicious because the bank risks losing a customer. If, however, he decides not to report an activity, he then has to convince the regulators that the transaction is not a suspicious one. One MLRO, for example, keeps a *"contemporaneous record"* of his judgement to defend his actions. An interesting relationship is that banks do not care if an MLRO decides not to reportan activity, and regulators do not usually care if MRLO reports an activity. *Defending* is, however, done mostly for not reporting an activity since MLROs are mostly aligned with banks as such, they may not report activities that would significantly upset customers with the consequent effect on profitability. But for MLROs that align with regulators and report SARs, they have to be prepared to defend their actions to management.

Finally, the *reporting line* of an MLRO partly determines if he is *playing safe, defending* himself or *reporting* to comply. Internal reporting to board and management that have good *culture* would make *playing safe* and *defending* less of a strategy; otherwise *playing safe* and *defending* will increase. External reporting to tough regulators that are committed to compliance would result in high *playing safe* and *defending* when the MLRO is aligned with the bank that has a conflicting interest with regulators.

Learning as a Property of Discharging

Learning is mainly used to deal with *unfair pressure* due to *shifting expectation*. It has two major properties: *training* and *networking*. Since *shifting expectation* is one of the major regulatory concerns, *learning* is a major category of *discharging* and hence *self-protecting*.

Learning for *discharging* is, however, determined by the *interest* of MLROs, the *culture* in their banks and their *belief* in the system. Their *interest* can override their capability when they use their skills and knowledge to circumvent regulations. *Learning* to discharge is, however, different from *learning* to comply, because *learning* to discharge is what most MLROs are doing in order to protect themselves while *learning* to comply is what is expected of them to do base on regulators' expectation. There is a fine line between the two, but it is the *intention* of MLROs that determine whether they are *learning* to discharge or *learning* to comply.

Training as a Property of Learning

There are two properties of *training*: *self-training* and *training others*. In *self-training*, MLROs are trying to make sure that they have the knowledge, skill and experience to be able to handle the pressure mainly from *shifting expectation.* They also need employees to have AML training, since their subordinates support them in *assessing* and *reporting* and *marginal employees* assist them in identifying suspicious activities.

Self-training is mostly informal. It includes reading a wide range of materials on regulations, enforcement actions, and information on changing laundering schemes. Finding relevant information, according to one MLRO, is one of the most important preoccupations of an MLRO. They also rely on alerts and money laundering forums for development in the industry. In one bank, they have an officer whose main duty is to search for information that would help their AML activities from all over the world and present his summary to the MLRO and his team.

Training others is, however, mostly formal and is usually conducted by the MLRO or an external consultant. Although it is done mainly to satisfy the expectation of regulators, it is a useful forum for an MLRO to emphasise the importance of AML issues to employees; to inform them of their obligation under the law and seek their cooperation and understanding. *Training others* is also closely related to *communicating* which is another concept used for *discharging.*

Networking as a Property of Learning

By far the most important way of *learning* for MLROs is through *networking.* They attend conferences, seminars and similar events not necessarily because of the training opportunity, but to share ideas with other MLROs that are in a similar situation. One way of *networking* is through *socialising.* MLROs are like a family; they socialise with each other to discuss how to deal with their problems, and get an opportunity for *complaining* about the *unfair pressure* of work. One MLRO, for example, stated that he usually invites his counterparts for lunch to discuss common problems and how to solve them. They also organise events, form associations and join anti-money laundering organisations to create opportunities for meeting their colleagues in other banks. This gives them the confidence to deal with *unfair pressure* from *shifting expectation* and *damage to reputation.*

Another form of *networking* is *collaborating* with internal and external stakeholders. MLROs rely heavily on the support of others to perform their duties effectively. Similarly, other compliance officers from different countries inform them of the situations in their domain: the new tricks, the regulation that would impact on their work and the way of resolving the concerns identified. This is, however, mainly for MLROs of banks that have an international operation, especially those in high-risk countries i.e. countries with high risks of money laundering activities. There is also an equally important *collaboration* with professional service firms, who provide information and assessing services. One of the services is a subscription-based package that entitles an MLRO to call for assistance in assessing a transaction, provide information on best practices and strategies on how others are dealing with similar situations. One MLRO said, it is the best investment he has made as an MLRO.

Automating as a Property of Discharging

Automating in this sense is the use of specialised software for *assessing* and *reporting* suspicious activities. It is used in *assessing* to protect the MLRO against concerns resulting from *shifting expectation* and *defective regulation* relating mainly to concern over the *watch list.*

An MLRO may not believe that *automating* is necessary, especially for one that is working in a bank that has fewer transactions like an MLRO of a private bank. Even for those in retail banks that consider it necessary, many believe it is not the solution for *assessing* suspicious activities. One MLRO that believes it is necessary, but not necessarily efficient is a veteran MLRO that said "*common sense*" is best for *assessing* suspicious activities. As a result of the role of *automating* in AML, a concept called *"unnecessary necessity"* was discovered to represent this idea, which means that since regulators are expecting MLROs to use specialised software for *assessing* and *reporting*, an MLRO has to have it even if he does not believe it is necessary. In this way, it is used for avoiding *punishment* from the regulators who may conclude that an MLRO that does not use specialised software is not committed to AML. An example of this was highlighted by the MLRO mentioned above who recalled a visit from the regulators. The regulators asked them whether they were using monitoring software and when the MLRO answered in the affirmative, the regulators were satisfied. He was surprised that they did not ask follow-up questions about the number of alerts and efficiency of the system.

The circumstances of regulation and the requirement of law is what make *automating* necessary since without AML software, it would be almost impossible for an MLRO of a big bank to be able to assess the volume of transactions that occur daily in his bank. For an MLRO of a big retail bank, it is a "*be all and end all*" of *assessing* and *reporting*, but not so for some MLROs of private banking and investment banking. MLROs of small banks believe that automation is more suited to the ruled-based approach rather than *risk-based approach* to compliance. There is, however, a consensus in data that *automating* is one of the best ways of *protecting* oneself from *unfair pressure* from the regulators. "*You cannot do without it*" was the conclusion of one MLRO.

Automating has other properties; it can be used to conspire to commit a money laundering offence when a dishonest MLRO colludes with management to hide suspicious transactions of valued customers. It also aids excessive *reporting* because of the ease with which transactions can be assessed, rightly or wrongly, as suspicious activities. *Automating* is, therefore, a means to an end, which is to protect rather than to prevent.

Complaining as a Property of Discharging

Complaining is a multidimensional concept. In addition to being a property of *discharging* when dealing with *regulatory concerns* and *communicating* when dealing with *organisational concerns*, it also indicates the alignment of an MLRO and the dimension of pressure, whether fair or unfair. In this section, *complaining* will be discussed as a property of *discharging* and later in the chapter it will be discussed as a property of *communicating*.

One way of dealing with *regulatory concern* is through *complaining* about the unfairness of regulation, the naivety of regulators, *damage to reputation* and *shifting expectation*. If one reflects back on those concerns discussed under the section on *unfair pressure*, then these are the same issues that MLROs complain about.

MLROs complain, for example, about the ineffectiveness, increased costs and lack of implementation of the *risk-based approach*. They complain about the prescriptive nature of regulations and unnecessary administrative burden of implementing regulations on *watch list*. Other complaints range from customer review necessitated by a change in regulation and monitoring of unstructured and from an inconsistent *watch list*. They also complain about regulators issuing blanket guidance without considering that there are different types of banks with a different nature and level of operation. Another complaint is that the MLROs that are trying to comply are at a disadvantage because regulators may not penalise an MLRO in one bank who did not report a certain customer, but would penalise an MLRO in another bank who erroneously gives a faulty report on the same customer.

Lack of feedback is another feature in their complaints; they would prefer a system that is more open and cooperative with a focus on information sharing and intelligence gathering. There are also a lot of complaints about the focus on systems and controls rather than concentrating on stopping money launderers from laundering money through the banking system. There are also those that complain about the UK as a haven for money laundering because of an apparently lax sentencing regime. An MLRO gives an example of China, where white collar criminals are sentenced to death for corruption, but in the UK a similar offence would not attract more than a few years that would even be suspended after a year or two in jail.

In addition to the above complaints, there is also the complaint about the increasing risk of prosecution and penalties because of the increased rhetoric of regulators on the back the recent money laundering scandals involving some of the big banks in the industry. Again, some MLROs complain about loss of reputation that may occur from unfavourable reports in the media that are painting MLROs as either incompetent or worse as criminals. According to one MLRO, for example, papers write "*as if banks and MLROs are the money launderers*". Furthermore, there is the constant complain about the *shifting expectation* of regulators. An MLRO is asked to use the *risk-based approach*, for example, but then he is implicitly expected to follow the guidance. Another complaint is the inflexibility of regulators; MLROs commented that they cannot possibly identify all suspicious transactions from the multitude of transactions that occur daily in their banks with limited resources available, but they are not allowed to use their *discretion* when *assessing* transactions. And finally, there is the concern that regulators do not have enough resources to supervise banks: they do not have enough employees, even for the employees that are available they are not skilled enough, and some do not have experience because of the regular staff turnover.

Complaining is, therefore, used by MLROs to deal with *unfair pressure* by letting out their frustration since there is little they can do to change the situation. *"What do you do?" was* the complaint of one MLRO who has to deal with conflicting pressure from regulators and customers relating to consent regime. They cannot complain to the regulators because they are required to comply and they cannot also complain to the banks because they are paid to deal with those issues. An MLRO, therefore, releases this frustration by talking to sympathetic ears of fellow MLROs, friends or interested parties.

Communicating as a Means of Self-protecting

Communicating is the next strategy for dealing with *unfair pressure* coming from the side of the bank from *under resources* and *marginal management*. It has three sub categories, namely *dialogue, justifying* and *threat*.

The *interest* of an MLRO determines the level of his communication. Even though most MLROs align with banks as discussed earlier, it may be in their own *interest* to confront them when necessary, especially when the *culture* in the organisations is weak. This is because the risk of *punishment* and damage to their reputation may be so high as to offset any immediate *reward* from the bank.

As a result of the interplay between *reward* and *punishment*, MLROs are more aggressive in their communication within the bank when their *interest* is at stake. In addition, the *culture* in an organisation as well as the level of *upstanding* of MLROs determines the level of their communication. A good *culture* breeds cooperative communication and bad *culture* breeds aggressive communication. Their *beliefs* also inform their decisions. An MLRO may not be aggressive in *communicating* when he believes, along with the bank, that AML regulations are unfair on the bank and customers.

Dialogue as a Property of Communicating

Dialogue is the primary method of dealing with unfair organisational pressure from *under resources* and *marginal management*. It has *negotiating* and *coordinating* as its properties.

MLROs are continually trying to negotiate for resources from management, negotiate with support staff, such as IT managers, for access to shared resources and persuade relationship and marketing managers to consider AML when performing their duties. *Marginal employees* are, however, usually profit oriented; they are more concerned with their *"bonuses"* than preventing money laundering. A relationship manager is more concerned about how to open more accounts and maintain customer relationship since he is judged on how well he meets his profit target. Similarly, a marketing manager wants to develop as many products and services as possible that would increase the bank's profitability. In both cases, they are less concerned with making sure that customers and products are not a source of money laundering. Managements are also more inclined towards profitability than preventing money laundering, although being also responsible for AML, they are mindful of the requirement of the law regarding AML regulation. Their primary objective is, however, to provide returns to shareholders and in the process benefit from enhanced remuneration and career development. Even though most marginal employees are profit oriented, customer-facing employees (clerks) are often not necessarily more concerned with profit at the expense of compliance.

By comparison, MLROs are, by definition, compliance oriented. They are appointed, in the eyes of regulators, primarily to assist in preventing money laundering; and in the eyes of banks to protect it from this risk of non-compliance with AML regulations. So an MLRO is supposed to be primarily concerned with complying with regulations to prevent money laundering and to reduce the impact of money laundering on the bank's operations. To balance this seemingly conflicting interest between the objectives of an MLRO and objectives of marginal employees, an MLRO has to be good at *negotiating*. It is, therefore, not easy for an MLRO to prevent relationship and marketing managers from opening new accounts and developing new products with associated risks of money laundering. One MLRO highlighted this issue when he stated that there is of course the usual pull between the marketing side and the compliance side, but sometime an MLRO has to compromise.

It is also not easy to convince management to adequately fund the operations of an MLRO function, to recruit more employees to assist the MLRO and to provide funding for the purchase of specialist software for *accessing* and *reporting*. In addition to being an additional cost without tangible financial benefit, the action of an MLRO may discourage existing customers from continuing their relationship with the bank and would possibly prevent new customer from joining the bank. The *reporting line* also influences the level of negotiation that an MLRO conducts. In some banks, an MLRO reports to a profit-oriented manager in corporate risk departments, for example, while in other banks, they report to a compliance-oriented managers in the legal departments. As a result, an MLRO that reports to a business-oriented manager would have more *negotiating* to do than an MLRO that reports to a compliance-oriented manager.

Coordinating is the other property of dialogue that deals with concerns about *marginal management*. In this case, an MLRO is dealing with different units within the bank and different people in other countries especially for a bank with international operation. An MLRO may be dealing with fraud, operational and legal departments. He may also be dealing with other compliance officers outside the UK. Thus, he is constantly sharing and receiving information from others to provide an update and to be up-to-date. He communicates changes in regulation and the impact of the changes to the bank and receives information about new money laundering innovations and changes in regulation in other jurisdictions that have an impact on his activities. He also communicates with the board and management informing them of their obligation and responsibility under changing regulations. It follows that *communicating* with different stakeholders is one of the most important parts of an MLRO's job.

In conclusion, the benefits of coordination for an MLRO are many. Keeping employees and management aware of changing regulations and recent developments would bring them closer to MLROs and by keeping them informed, an MLRO will easily gain their support in implementing difficult decisions. An MLRO can also provide evidence that he is performing his duties as expected by regulators and the bank. Besides, MLROs also benefit from information on money laundering innovations and international developments to assist them in discharging their responsibilities.

Justifying as a Property of Communicating

The next property after *dialogue* is *justifying*. MLROs have to justify the need for resources, and they have to justify their decisions because it affects profitability.

The first and most important is *justifying* the need for resources for investment in technology. As seen earlier in section "Protecting as a Means of Resolving the Main Concern", technology is a necessity, especially for MLROs in retail banking. They need it to protect themselves against unfair pressure from regulators. Justifying the need to purchase a new or to upgrade existing software is, therefore, one of the most important preoccupations of MLROs. As a result, they gather evidence from all sources to show why it is important, invite software providers to inform them of the benefits of new technology, take advantage (and sometimes even hope for, according to one participant) scandals in the industry to push for the need to protect the bank from becoming a victim. MLROs also need to justify their worth to their banks. They need to justify why they should be promoted and also why they need more staff to support them. One MLRO of an investment bank complained that he was the only person in his bank that deals with all AML issues, though he said he understood why banks are reluctant in spending money on AML.

Justifying is also related to the negative impact on profitability of some decisions of MLROs. A decision advising against establishing a relationship with a customer or rejecting a new product or service because of the risk of money laundering, for example, is going to affect the profitability of the bank. An MLRO, therefore, has to justify his decision with convincing arguments. Besides, it is also in the interest of the MLRO to increase the profitability of the bank, so it is not a decision they take lightly as seen when discussing the concept of *balancing* earlier, where an MLRO would weigh the cost and benefit of each decision before deciding whether to report or not to report. One of the MLROs explicitly admitted that, in the end, he has to determine what is good for the bank because ultimately they are the ones that pay his salary. He added "*I am an employee of the bank, I will therefore naturally align with them*".

Threat as a Property of Communicating

The next sub-category of *communicating* is *threat*. It is the last resort of an MLRO when dealing with *organisational concerns*.

MLROs sometimes threaten staff and even management when the pressure of *under resources* and *marginal management* becomes unbearable. They "*encourage*" (subtle threat) front officers to identify and report unusual transaction by informing them of the consequences of not reporting. Similarly, they threaten profit-oriented staff with the risk of prosecution if they conspire with a customer to launder money. They may also report employees that fail to support them to management who will then direct staff to comply. In addition, some implicitly threaten management to give them the resources they need to perform their duties since management knows that they have direct access to regulators. Some MLROs also keep records of any disagreement in case the issue should come up during a regulatory visit with the purpose of shifting blame to the management. In extreme circumstances, a few will threaten to resign and allow management to explain the reason for their resignation. One of the MLROs was very clear about resigning; he had told his superiors that he would resign and inform regulators about his decision if they compromise his position.

The alignment of an MLRO would, however, soften the need for threat. If MLROs' interests align with that of the bank that has a weak *culture*, they may not be concerned in which case most of their *protecting* would be against the *unfair pressure* from regulators. If, however, their *interests* are more aligned with that of regulators because of their *upstanding*, background or the high risk of punishment, for example, then the level of threat would increase and *resigning* and whistle blowing would be viable options.

Complaining as a Property of Communicating

This book has demonstrated how *complaining* is used as a property of *discharging*, but it is also a property of *communicating* dealing with *unfair pressure* from the bank though it is a much lower level that it being a property of *discharging*.

One of the areas that MLROs complain much about is *lack of resources*. On the one hand, regulators are putting pressure on MLROs to perform their duties and, on the other hand, banks are not willing to provide adequate resources. MLROs also complain about the lack of management support and lack of cooperation from other marginal employees. *Complaining* is, therefore, high in banks that have bad culture that encourage profit at the expense of compliance.

The *shifting expectation* of regulators, lack of resources and lack of support increases the perception of unfairness by MLROs. Under this intense pressure, some MLROs contemplate resigning since there is nothing they can do about it. One MLRO said that *"I know of few people who have resigned their job because they could not tolerate what was happening"*. *Resigning* is, however, an option that is rarely exercised because it would not best serve the interest of an MLRO who may find it difficult to find another job.

Theory Discovery

Having explained the various concepts that make the main concern of *unfair pressure* and how it is being resolved through *self-protecting*, the following section discusses how the core category and the main concern are combined to form the theory of *self-protecting*.

The Emergence of the Self-protecting Theory

This section explains how the theory emerged from the data based on the concepts discussed in the previous sections. The *self-protecting* theory states that the more *unfair pressure* is placed on MLROs, the more they *protect* themselves rather that *prevent* money laundering. This theory represents a continuum between *preventing* money laundering and *protecting* self. While the intention of regulators is to prevent money laundering, the unfair nature of some pressure on MLROs is leaving them with no option than to protect themselves instead of assisting in *preventing money* laundering.

The theory is derived from the degree family of theoretical codes that represent theories dealing with range, extreme, intensity, extent and polarity. The degree code is also supported by binary code that belongs to the "*paired opposite family*" of theoretical codes. These codes formed the foundation of the theory with the intensity of *unfair pressure* representing the degree family and the polarity between prevention and protection representing the paired opposite theoretical code. Not only are these two codes represented in the main theory, but they are also represented in the main concepts of the theory as seen earlier. We have, for example, *regulatory concerns and organisational concerns; discharging* and *complying; communicating* and *cooperation* as some manifestation of the codes.

In summary, the theory is suggesting that a high *unfair pressure* means that an MLRO is *self-protecting*, but a low *unfair pressure* means that an MLRO is *preventing* money laundering. *Protecting* is, however, not necessarily in relation to *unfair pressure* from the regulators. In a situation when the interest of banks and the regulators conflict, an MLRO that is *aligning* with regulators to prevent money laundering would be *protecting* himself against *unfair pressure* from the bank instead of *preventing* the bank from losing income.

The following diagrams show the main concerns and how they are resolved as discussed in the previous sections (Fig. 3.1).

The basic form of the theory, based on the discussion above, is: the more *unfair pressure* on individuals the more they protect themselves. There are several examples outside the substantive area of money

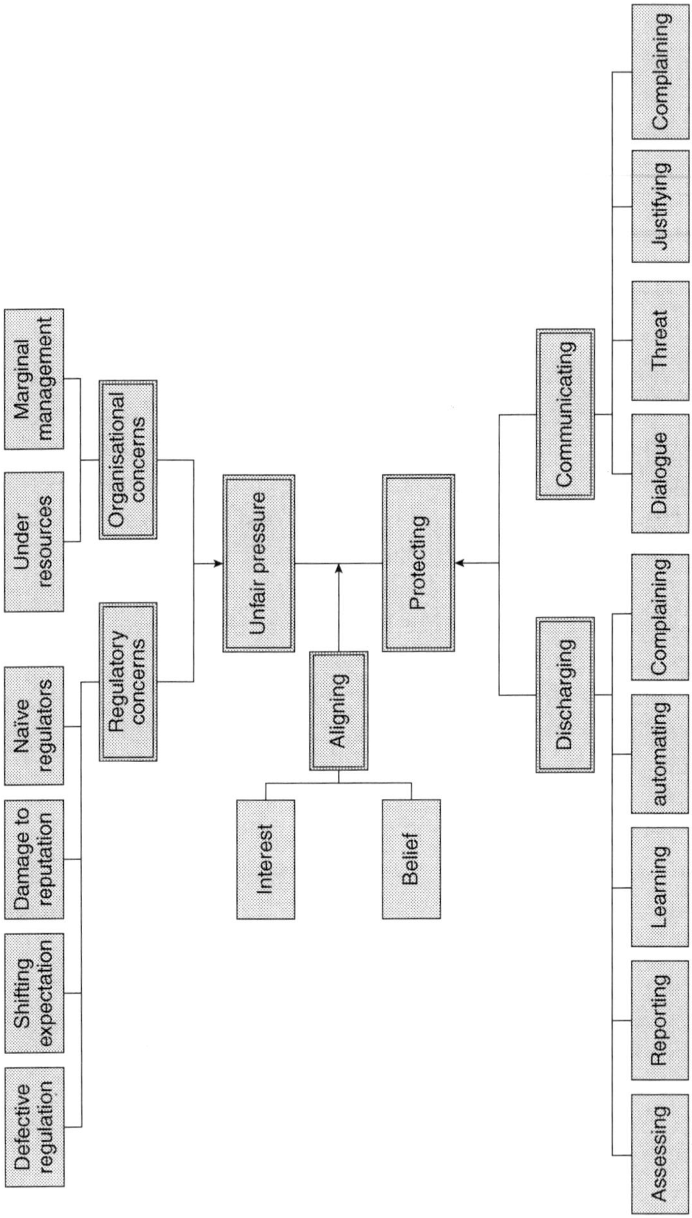

Fig. 3.1 Summary of concerns and categories

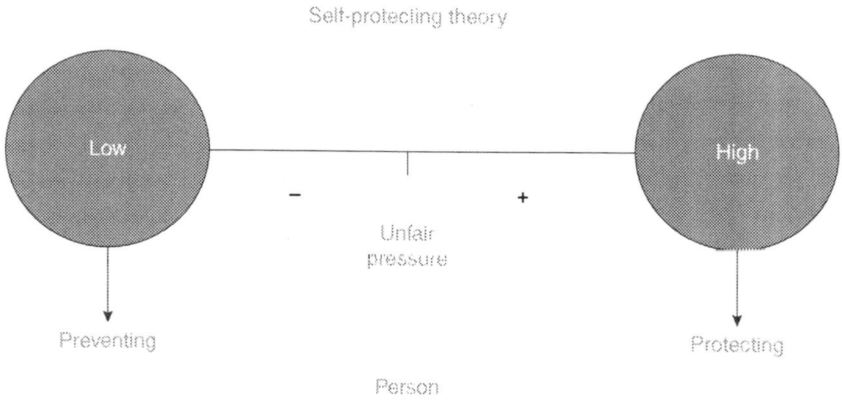

Fig. 3.2 The basics of self-protecting

laundering to support this theory, and this would be explained in the chapter on the general implication of the theory.

The basic theory can be depicted using the following diagram (Fig. 3.2).

As discussed earlier, MLROs are *self-protecting* either by *discharging* or *communicating*. They are *discharging* to deal with *regulatory concerns* and *communicating* to deal with *organisational concerns*. The data is, however, showing that much of what is happening within the UK banking industry is that MLROs are *aligning* with banks and *discharging* their responsibilities. This assertion is evident if we consider the discussion on *unfair pressure, aligning* and *complaining*.

It was seen earlier in the chapter that most of the *unfair pressure* comes from *regulatory concerns* related to *defective regulation, naïve regulators, shifting expectation* and *damage to reputation* on the side of the regulators as compared to *unfair pressure* from *under resources* and *marginal management* on the side of the bank. It follows from the discussion that the source of *unfair pressure* is the regulators.

The concepts of *aligning* and *complaining* also clearly suggest the position of an MLRO in the UK. As discussed earlier in the chapter, MLROs are mainly *complaining* against *unfair pressure* from regulators rather that *complaining* about the *unfair pressure* from banks. They are also more aligned with banks than they are with regulators since the more an MLRO is *complaining* against one party that is the source of *unfair pressure,* the more he is *aligning* with the other.

In the light of this discovery, the theory is, therefore, suggesting that MLROs in the UK are mainly *discharging* their responsibilities to *protect* themselves rather that complying with regulation to *prevent* money laundering.

This can be represented by the following diagram.

The theory, as discovered within the research, is, however, flexible. In a country where *unfair pressure* is coming from banks and MLROs are aligning with the regulators, for example, an MLRO would be *communicating* to protect himself rather that *cooperating* to prevent money laundering.

In this situation where MLROs are mainly *communicating* to protect themselves, the discovered theory explains this hypothetical situation by stating that the more *unfair pressure* on MLROs from banks the more they are *communicating* to protect themselves rather that cooperating to prevent money laundering. *Communicating*, as in seen the chapter, means increased level of *dialogue, justifying* and *threat* to protect themselves against *unfair pressure* from banks while *cooperating* through information sharing and intelligence gathering is the "*paired opposite*" of *communicating* just like *complying* is the "*paired opposite*" of *discharging*. This is a manifestation of the paired opposite theoretical code discussed in Chap. 1 on methodology, suggesting that the presence of one implies the presence of the other, that is, *discharging* suggests *complying* and *communicating* suggests *cooperating*, just like *protecting* suggests *preventing*. There is, however, a thin line between these paired opposite concepts, but the data is showing that, in the UK at least, *discharging, communicating* and *protecting* are more grounded than *complying*, co-*operation* and *preventing* as seen previously.

This hypothetical situation can be depicted as follows.

Self-protecting Framework

In addition to generating a theory, one of the aims of the research (Chap.1) was to discover a framework that would assist in the evaluation of the level of AML compliance. Looking at the two scenarios above in which MLROs that are *aligning* with banks are *discharging* their responsibility to protect themselves and MLROs that are *aligning* with regulators are *communicating* to protect themselves, a framework was discovered. The framework seeks to explain the behaviours of MLROs and nature of regulation in a particular country. Person, regulation and location are three conceptions that can be explained by the framework as will be seen in the following paragraphs.

The construction of the theory shows that, on the one hand, an MLROs that align with the bank and is under *unfair pressure* from the regulators are *discharging* their responsibility to protect themselves (Fig. 3.3). The opposite also applies: an MLRO that aligns with regulators and is under fair pressure from the bank would be *complying* with regulation to prevent money laundering. On the other hand, an MLRO that is aligned with the regulators and is under *unfair pressure* from the bank is *communicating* to protect himself (Fig. 3.4). The opposite also applies; an MLRO that aligns with the bank and is under fair pressure from regulators would be *cooperating* with regulators to *preventing* money laundering.

It should be noted that by *aligning* with one party, it does not mean that an MLRO is not under any *unfair pressure* at all from that party, but

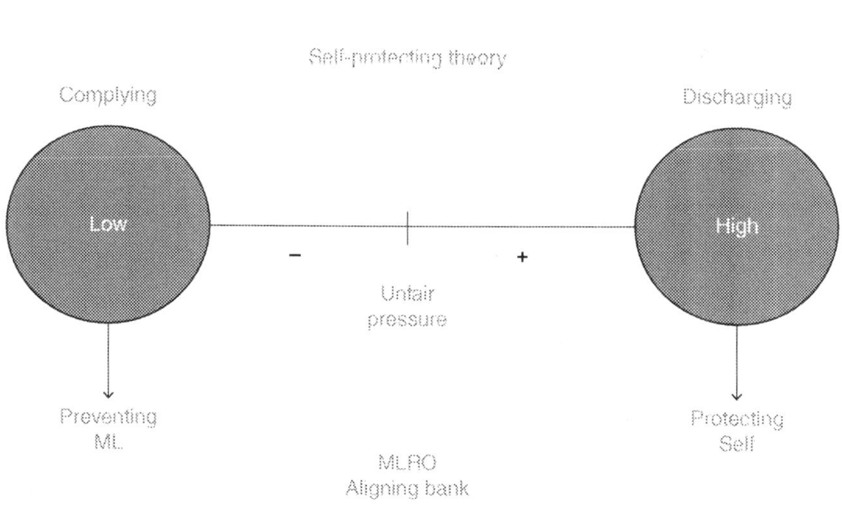

Fig. 3.3 The self-protecting theory (complying vs discharging)

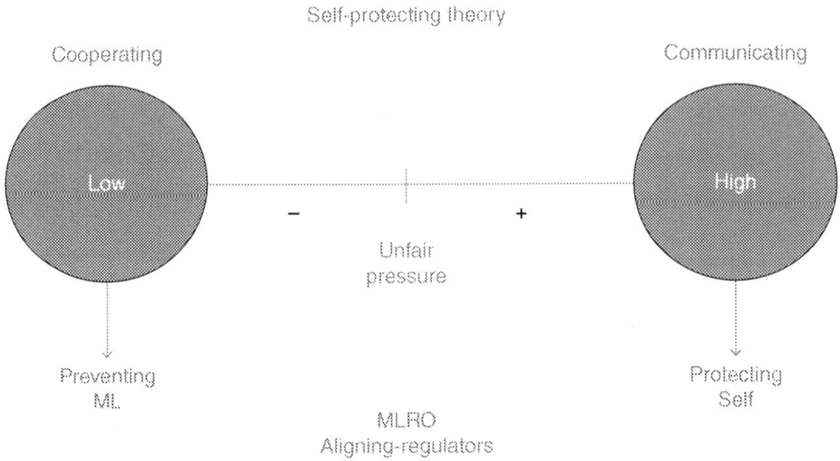

Fig. 3.4 The self-protecting theory (cooperating vs communicating)

rather the *unfair pressure* is much lower than the one coming from the other party they are not *aligning* with. That is why even though MLROs in the UK are aligning with banks rather regulators, they still have to deal with *unfair pressure* from *under resources* and *marginal management* by *communicating*.

This in essence is the self-protecting framework and can be depicted as follows (Fig. 3.5).

Location

As stated earlier, MLROs in the UK belong mainly to the *discharging* quadrant that is they are *aligning* with banks and are under *unfair pressure* mainly from regulators. As such, they are mainly *discharging* their responsibilities to protect themselves. It may be that, in another country, MLROs are *aligning* with regulators and under *unfair pressure* from banks and are, therefore, *communicating* to protect themselves. Further research in other jurisdictions would confirm in which quadrant each country is located.

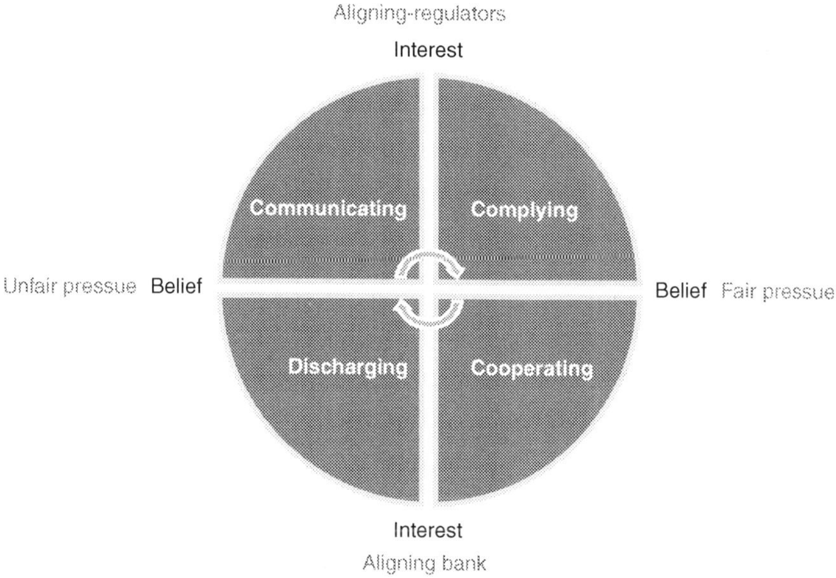

Fig. 3.5 The self-protecting framework

Person

Even within a single jurisdiction, such as the UK, some MLROs are *aligning* with regulators to protect themselves against the bank, although the majority are *aligning* with the bank to protect themselves against the regulators. An example of this from the data was an MLRO that lost his job for whistle blowing against the bank and another who said *"what I usually tell my managers is that if you compromise my position I will resign, and I will inform [name of regulator] about it"*. Therefore, an MLRO that aligns himself with a bank and is under *unfair pressure* from regulators will belong to the *discharging* quadrant, and an MLRO that aligns with regulators and is under *unfair pressure* from a bank will belong to the *communicating* quadrant. Similarly, an MLRO that aligns with regulators and is under fair pressure from a bank will be in the *complying* quadrant, and an MLRO that aligns with a bank and is under fair pressure from the regulators will belong to the *cooperating* quadrant.

Regulation

The framework can also be used to explain the nature of regulation. The *Discharging* quadrant may represent *weak regulation*, since the MLROs are aligning with banks, not necessarily because of fair pressure from the bank but because of *unfair pressure* from regulators. Likewise, the *Communicating* quadrant represents *tough regulation* since MLROs are *aligning* with regulators, despite the certain *reward* from banks. This suggests that the uncertain *punishment* from regulators is becoming more certain since, according to one participant, "*I, however, think enforcement will increase because the regulators said so. [Name of person] was clear that they are going to increase enforcement action. You are going to see a lot of fines*". In the same way, the *Complying* quadrant may represent *smart regulation* since MLROs are still *aligning* with regulators, but are receiving fair pressure from banks maybe because of regulators' constructive attitude towards banks. Finally, the *Cooperating* quadrant may represent *self-regulation* since the theory is suggesting that MLROs are *aligning* banks and are under fair pressure from regulators, maybe because of the *cooperative* attitude of banks towards regulators.

The following diagram shows how location, person and regulation can be explained within the framework (Fig. 3.6).

The framework shows that the regulation in the UK is weak because most MLROs are mainly discharging their responsibilities to protect themselves rather complying with regulation to prevent money laundering as discussed earlier.

Determinants

The presence of *belief* and *interest* in the framework signifies their effect on *aligning* and fairness of pressure. If the *interests* of MLROs align with the *interest* of the bank or are best served by the bank, then they align with the bank. If, however, the *interests* of MLROs align with that of regulators, then they align with regulators.

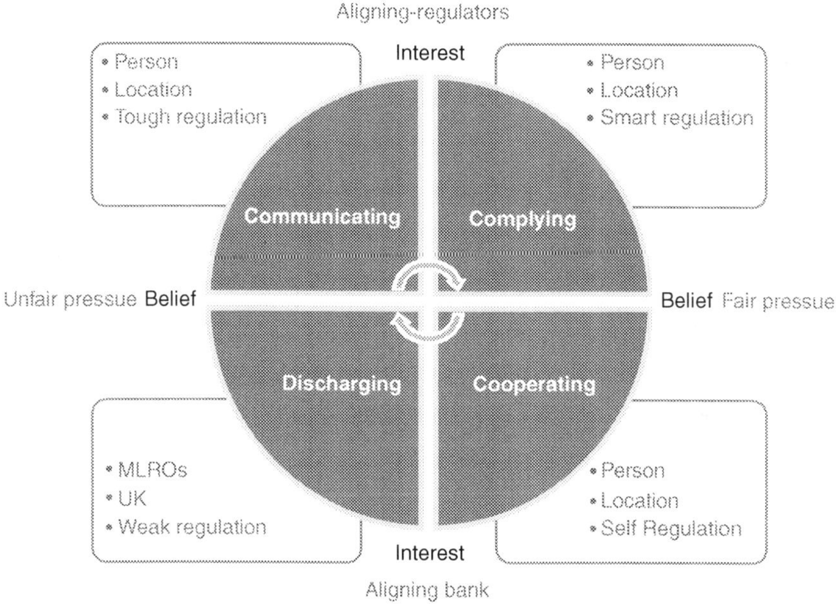

Fig. 3.6 Detailed self-protecting framework

In addition to being a property of alignment, *belief* is also a strong indicator of what is fair and what is unfair as discussed earlier in the chapter. When an MLRO *believes* that a pressure is unfair, then it does not matter if regulators or a bank believes otherwise; his behaviour would be either *discharging* or *communicating* depending on his alignment. If, however, he *believes* that pressure is fair, his behaviour would either be *complying* or *cooperating*, again depending on his alignment.

The framework is, therefore, a useful tool that can be used to identify the behaviour of MLROs and the nature of regulations in a country.

Conclusion

The theory of *self-protecting*, although derived from the substantive area of money laundering, has general implications. *Protecting* oneself because of *unfair pressure* occurs in several organisations including hospitals, schools and businesses. In nursing, for example, there is a pull and push on nurses by authorities on one side and patients on the other; doctors also have to contend with conflicting pressures from regulators on one hand and patients on the other. The same applies in schools, where teachers are torn between following school regulations and imparting knowledge to students. It is even more pronounced in companies where employees with marginal responsibility, like auditors and compliance officers, are facing conflicting pressure from management on one hand and regulators on the other mainly because of the conflicting interests between the two. The list is endless because a grounded theory has a general implication and is abstract of time, place and people.

Consequently, *self-protecting* theory's potential contribution to knowledge is immense. *Self-protecting* theory is not only applicable to other disciplines, but its main concepts are also applicable to other areas. The concept of *marginal management*, for example, can be used in management research to explain the difficulty of managing people not under a person's direct control; the concept of *automating* can be used to explain the reasons why, despite the problem of "*big data*", technology is still the preferred way of analysing data. The concept of *shifting expectation* also captures a view of expectation that is novel. Furthermore, the concept of *complaining* as an indicator of *unfair pressure* can be used for defining fairness in general. There is also *aligning* which is a high-level concept that can be used to show the direction of allegiances of an individual. This is useful not only to organisations, but also to countries that are interested in gauging public opinion on a matter of national interest.

The opportunity for further research is also abundant. The concept of *marginal management, aligning, shifting expectation, complaining* and others can be the basis of further research in various fields of endeavours. The *self-protecting* theory can also be tested using quantitative methodology using the *self-protecting* framework to verify the theory in different countries starting with the UK. Similarly, a theory can be discovered about the concerns of regulators which will then be combined with this theory to find a common ground. There is also the possibility of discovering a formal theory by combining the *self-protecting* theory with similar theories in other fields to discover a more comprehensive theory.

In conclusion, the *self-protecting* theory aptly captures the behaviour of MLROs in the UK on how they are dealing with their main concern of unfair pressure. The theory's main contribution is that it fits; it is relevant, it is workable and it is modifiable. It also has general implications and is a source for further study in the substantive areas of money laundering and beyond.

In this chapter, the *Self-protecting* theory was presented together with how it emerged from the data. The main concern of *unfair pressure* was discussed and the way of resolving the concern through *self-protecting* was explained before integrating the various concepts into the *self-protecting* theory. Finally, a framework for AML compliance discovered from the theory was also presented.

4

Compliance and Regulatory Dilemma

Introduction

This chapter reviews the literature on regulation in general, highlights the problems within the literature and then relates the discussion to AML regulation and compliance.

The *self-protecting* theory is more of a sociological theory because the main concern that was identified, *unfair pressure*, is found more in social theory literature, and the classical grounded theory methodology adopted for the research underpinning this book has its root in sociology (Glaser & Strauss 1965). Interestingly, however, the outcome is similar in some respect to economic theory of regulation. In fact, the *self-protecting* framework discovered from the theory is similar to the game theory's application to regulation as described in Scholz (1984). In this regard, the work of Becker (1968) and Scholz (1984) will be reviewed to show the link between the *self-protecting* theory and the economic theory of regulation.

Most importantly, however, the theory also explains compliance from the perspective of social theory. The social theory of Tyler (2006) on

A.U. Bello, *Improving Anti-Money Laundering Compliance,*
Palgrave Studies in Risk, Crime and Society,
DOI 10.1007/978-3-319-43264-9_4

legitimacy will also be reviewed to show the linkage. The chapter will also look at the combination of social and economic theories in resolving the dichotomy between the two schools of thought. This approach has also been the subject of research in the field of regulation. Example of some studies that used this approach include Sutinen and Kuperan (1999) on socio-economic theory of regulation and Ayres and Braithwaite (1992) on responsive regulation.

Essentially, the problem of regulation and compliance is to find the right balance between the effectiveness of regulation and the efficiency of compliance.

What Is Regulation?

The concept of regulation is *"historically as old as the notion of government"* (Ünay 2011 p. 23). It is a system designed to influence behaviour of individuals and firms (Friedman 1985; Scholz 1984) or as defined by Selznick (1985 p. 363), regulation is a *"sustained and focused control exercised by a public agency over activities that are valued by a community"*. Regulations was also explained "as *a specific set of commands . . . as deliberate state influence . . . and as all forms of social and economic influence"* (Baldwin & Cave 1999).

There are several reasons for regulation but the most common reason is to correct market failure (Baldwin & Cave 1999). According Prosser (2006), however, market failure rationale is inadequate and he argued that protection of human rights and to further social solidary are other justifications for regulation. Accordingly, the two main reasons for regulation are market failure rationale and rights-based social rationale (Baldwin & Cave 1999).

Problem of Regulation

The problem of regulation has been discussed extensively in the literature (Grabosky 1995). It is an age old problem of regulation and deregulation (Ayres & Braithwaite 1992; Kroszner & Strahan 1999; Scholz 1984) with proponents of each approach presenting theories to champion their causes. It is also an ideological debate, with conservatives generally preferring less regulation and liberals preferring more regulation (Ayres & Braithwaite 1992).

There is also a debate about the basis of regulation. The advocates of the economic theory of regulation, for instance, wish the issue to be seen purely in economic terms ignoring moral considerations (Geiger & Wuensch 2007; Sutinen & Kuperan 1999) while the social theorists contend that social issue are more important in determining compliances (Tyler 2006). There is also the debate about the public interest theory and the private interest theory relating to the issue of compliance (Kroszner & Strahan 1999).

While all these are legitimate debates, the one that the author found to be more interesting is the debate about the trade-off between efficiency and effectiveness (Masciandaro 1999). It is interesting because it ties in with the other debates since the proponents and opponents of each theory are looking for the most effective approach, the most efficient approach or an approach that strikes the right balance between efficiency and effectiveness.

In summary, the problem of regulation and compliance is to find the right balance between the effectiveness of regulation and the efficiency of compliance.

Effectiveness and Efficiency Consideration

Effectiveness has been defined as the ability to achieve an objective while efficiency is the effective utilization of resources to achieve that objective (P. Jackson 2012).

This definition is vital to the understanding of the contribution of self-protecting theory to regulation because, as argued in the book, there are two conflicting pressure that bear on an MLRO, and each party, that is banks and regulators have different objectives that make their view on efficiency and effectiveness different.

Interestingly, the idea of effectiveness and efficiency was discovered in a money laundering article on the economics of regulation (Masciandaro 1999), which highlighted the trade-off between effectiveness and efficiency in AML compliance. The article however looked at effectiveness in terms of reducing money laundering and efficiency as regard the cost to the regulated of complying with AML regulations. This book, however, is looking at the trade-off between regulators and effectiveness and efficiency from the point of view of the regulated.

The difference between the two concepts of effectiveness and efficiency can be explained by the following illustration. A process may be effective if a desired level of output is achieved, but may not be efficient if the cost of achieving it is higher than the benefit. Example of this in management is one view of the cost of quality (Garvin 1984); should a company spend vast amounts of resources to ensure a defect free product or should it allow some level of defect to ensure efficient use of resources? Relating this concept to regulation, Becker (1968) puts it succinctly: *"how many resources and how much punishment should be used to enforce different kinds of legislation?"*.

Those that argued for a higher level of regulation and view regulation from the point of view of public interest might be more concerned with effective enforcement, which is considered inherently inefficient (Grabosky 1995). Those that favour deregulation and view regulation from the private interest perspective may, however, be more concerned with efficient compliance, which might not be effective because of the problem of regulatory capture (Ayres & Braithwaite 1992), the tendency for private sector organisations to influence regulation for their own benefit. For those that favour a balanced approach, a cost of quality that minimises the total cost of quality is a fitting description of their approach. The middle course belongs to the balanced approach class that seeks to find the optimal level of regulation that strikes a balance between effectiveness and efficiency for each party involved (regulators and regulated).

And this is the balance that most researchers seek to achieve (Ayres & Braithwaite 1992; Becker 1968; Masciandaro 1999; Scholz 1984; Sutinen & Kuperan 1999). Within these groups of researchers are the economists, who are promoting the economic theory of regulation, and on the opposite side are the sociologists, who are promoting social theory of regulation. Then there are others promoting the combination of the two schools of thought in their desire to arrive at an optimal level.

In the first group is Becker (1968 p. 209) who proposed that an economic approach to regulation is better since *"optimal policies to combat illegal behaviour are part of an optimal allocation of resources"*. While the second group is represented by Tyler (2006 p. 270) argued that *"people's motivation to cooperate with others, in this case legal authorities, is rooted in social relationships and ethical judgments, and does not primarily flow from the desire to avoid punishments or gain rewards"*.

Relationship between Regulatory Theories and the Self-protecting Theory

At this point, it may be necessary to provide a summary of the various regulatory theories mentioned in the preceding section to provide a context for explaining the contribution of the middle course approach to regulation.

Economic Theory of Regulation

Becker (1968) was the first to formally develop a framework for explaining criminal behaviour (Sutinen & Kuperan 1999) with the application of the economist's usual analysis of choice to conclude that the *"optimal policies to combat illegal behaviour are part of an optimal allocation of resources"* (Becker 1968 p. 209). The economic approach therefore assumes that *"a person commits an offense if the expected utility to him exceeds the utility he could get by using his time and other resources at other activities"* (Becker 1968 p. 176).

This approach has been criticised for ignoring the part social theory plays in explaining compliance (Ayres & Braithwaite 1991; Scholz 1993; Sutinen & Kuperan 1999; Tyler 2006). Sutinen and Kuperan (1999) faulted the approach by saying that economic theory of regulation ignores evidence that shows compliance is also influenced by intangible motivations rather that tangible motivations alone, and therefore it is *"inadequate explanation of compliance behaviour"*. Similar criticism was pointed out by Ayres and Braithwaite (1991) who said that, *"most citizens comply with the law most of the time because it seems wrong to them to break the law".*

Becker's deterrence theory is, however, a seminal work that is the basis of economic theory of crime (Geiger & Wuensch 2007). What has remained dominant (Tyler 2006) is a testament to its relevance in explaining compliance behaviour. Part of the self-protecting theory is similar to this theory since *interest* was found to be a key concept that explains the aligning of an MLRO to either banks or regulators. The link is also evident if the properties of *interest* are considered. *Reward* and *punishment*, for example, are the two concepts discovered as the properties of *interest*, which suggests that an MLRO would align with the organisation that best serves his interest as seen in the previous chapter on self-protecting theory. This is similar to the self-interest concept of the economic theory which holds that an individual acts rationally to maximise his personal utility (Geiger & Wuensch 2007). Self-protecting theory however has social concepts called *belief* that complements the concept of *interest*, unlike in the economic theory that believe social theories are dispensable in explaining compliance behaviour (Becker 1968).

Social Theory of Regulation

Social theorists on the other hand hold that there is an alternative approach to regulation in which compliance behaviour is *"rooted in social relationships and ethics judgements, and does not primarily flow from the desire to avoid punishment or gain reward"* (Tyler 2006 p. 270). Tyler (2006) even argued that though in some cases the deterrence approach influences behaviour, in other instances, *"there is no significant influence of risk-related judgments on compliance with the law"* (Tyler 2006 p. 269).

The theory behind this argument is called legitimacy theory. The idea is that legitimacy is *"a state of widespread belief; namely, the belief that an order is obligatory or exemplary. Moreover, the belief is a reason for action"* (Hyde 1983 p. 382). By this definition therefore *"gaining the consent and cooperation of the public with the law and legal authorities"* (Tyler 2006 p. 270) is a better approach for ensuring compliance. Other social theories include the cognitive theory that recognised the place of morality in determining compliance behaviour and social learning theory that states that peer pressure and social influence determines compliance behaviour (Sutinen & Kuperan 1999).

This and similar approaches were however seen by Becker (1968 p. 176) as irrelevant in explaining criminal behaviour since according to him *"Some persons become 'criminals', therefore, not because their basic motivation differs from that of other persons, but because their benefits and costs differ"*. Hyde (1983 p. 385) also discounted legitimacy when he stated that *"I am convinced that the Weberian model-law to belief to behaviour – at best is problematic and unproven and at worst is probably wrong"*.

Self-protecting theory however accepts the value of belief in shaping behaviour. The concept of *belief* generated in the research, which has *ethics, culture* and *conviction* as it properties, is in line with the idea of legitimacy discussed by Weber, Roth, and Wittich (1978 p. 31), in which *"action, especially social action which involves a social relationship, may be guided by the belief in the existence of a legitimate order"*. Furthermore, the concept of procedural justice in legitimacy theory is aligned with *unfair pressure* since *"people are widely found to react to the fairness by which authorities and institutions make decisions and exercise authority, and these reactions shape both their willingness to accept decisions"* (Tyler 2006 p. 273). However, *self-protecting* theory also agrees with the concept of self-interest represented by the two concepts of *reward* and *punishment*, the properties of *interest* discussed earlier.

It is interesting that Hyde (1983) mentioned self-interest and belief as two distinct concepts for explaining behaviour. This suggests the fitness of the two concepts of *interest* and *belief* generated in this research as shown in the self-protecting framework discussed in the previous chapter. In the framework, *belief* determines the perception of pressure to be either fair or unfair while *interest* is a concept that determines the alignment of an MLRO. These two concepts according to the self-protecting theory determine the compliance behaviour of an MLRO.

Socio-economic Theory

In trying to reconcile the economic and social view of regulation, several researchers have proposed theories for effective regulation.

Notably research relevant to this study are Scholz (1984), Ayres and Braithwaite (1992) and Sutinen and Kuperan (1999) who tried to strike a balance between economic and social theory of regulation. Scholz (1984) presented the concept of regulatory game for enforcing regulation by building on the work of Axelrod (1980) on *"tit for tat"* approach based on the economic concept of game theory, while Ayres and Braithwaite (1992) significantly extended the work in responsive regulation to distance it further away from its economic foundation since the approach is primarily *"based on rational self-interest calculations"* (Scholz 1984 p. 385). There is also the social economic theory that introduced theories from *"psychology and sociology to account for both tangible and intangible motivations'* influencing compliance with regulations" (Sutinen & Kuperan 1999 p. 174).

Voluntary Compliance and Regulatory Enforcement

Scholz (1984 p. 388) voluntary compliance approach is an attempt to tackle the enforcement dilemma which feature is *"that mutual suspicions may lead to confrontation between regulator and regulated firms, even when firm, agency, and society as a whole would be better off with voluntary compliance and cooperative enforcement"*. This dilemma is common in regulation and enforcement situations (Scholz 1984) and AML is not an exception. This supports the premise of the self-protecting theory, which suggests that there is conflicting interest between banks and regulators that result in pressure on MLROs to align with either one or the other.

In trying to resolve this conflict, Scholz (1984 p. 385) proposed the adoption of a strategy that would encourage "*voluntary compliance*" using "*tit for tat*" strategy that "*requires agencies to be reasonable toward cooperative firms, vengeful toward cheaters, unrelenting in pursuit of chronic evaders, but conciliatory toward repentant firm*". The strategy is based on the prisoner's dilemma in which if prisoners:

> Both cooperate, both do fairly well. But if one defects while the other cooperates, the defecting side gets its highest payoff, and the

> cooperating side is the sucker and gets its lowest payoff. This gives both sides an incentive to defect. The catch is that if both do defect, both do poorly. (Axelrod 1980 p. 4)

Scholz (1984) identified four different situations based on the behaviour of the firms and the regulators that is, voluntary compliance, confrontation, temptation and harassment. According to Scholz (1984), when an agency and a firm cooperate (voluntary compliance), they both benefit from their strategies but when they engage in confrontational behaviour (confrontation), they both lose. Similarly, if one cooperates and the other fails to cooperate, the entity that fails to cooperate will benefit at the expense of the other (temptation—firms benefit; harassment—regulators benefit).

The similarities between these strategies and the self-protecting concepts of *cooperation*, *discharging*, *complying* and *communicating* may be evident at least in concept if not in content. The difference, however, is that apart from voluntary compliance, temptation and harassment which can be closely aligned to *cooperation*, *discharging* and *communicating* respectively, the other concept of confrontation is not aligned with *complying* though at a higher level of abstraction they can be related.

Based on this model, Scholz (1984) proposed that the optimal strategy is voluntary compliance, but other strategies can also be applied as necessary to ensure compliance. The middle course approach, however, differ from this conclusion and this would be discussed separately later in the chapter. It is pertinent, however, to highlight some of the criticism of the voluntary compliance by Ayres and Braithwaite (1992) who argued that the strategy necessarily lends itself to the problem of capture.

Responsive Regulation

Responsive regulation is the approach suggested by Ayres and Braithwaite (1992) to deal with the problem of "capture" they identified in voluntary compliance approach of Scholz (1984). They stated that "*the features of regulatory encounters that foster the evolution of cooperation often also encourage the evolution of capture and corruption"*. The problem of capture to Ayres and Braithwaite (1992 p. 54), is therefore the main problem for regulation (Mendeloff 1993). In trying to address the problem of capture, four strategies have been proposed: the benign big gun, republic tripartism, enforced self-regulation and partial industry intervention (Ayres & Braithwaite 1992).

Benign big gun is in line with the *"tit for tat"* approach in which regulatory agencies have a different way of dealing with regulated organisations that are *"contingently provocable and forgiving"* (Ayres & Braithwaite 1992 p. 19). Republic tripartism is however concerned with *"empowering public interest group"* to be part of the regulatory process (Ayres & Braithwaite 1992 p. 54). The enforced self-regulation is about negotiated regulatory standards between regulators and regulated while partial-industry intervention means regulating part of the industry and leaving the other part unregulated (Ayres & Braithwaite 1992). At least three of these strategies are also related to the *self-protecting* theory. Benign big gun, for example, may correspond to *complying*, and enforced self-regulation to *cooperating*. The concept of republican tripartism can also be located with the middle course approach to the extent that it also recognised the need for a third party, which in the case of self-protecting are the MLROs rather that public interest groups.

Unlike Scholz (1984) that recognises voluntary compliance as a better strategy, Ayres and Braithwaite (1992 p. 101) suggest that "*there is no such thing as an ahistorical optimal regulatory strategy"* but the appropriateness of a strategy depends on the circumstances under consideration. The multiple proposals of Ayres and Braithwaite (1992) were however questioned as was their inattention to the *"the distinction between effectiveness and efficiency"* (Mendeloff 1993). Other reviews, while acknowledging the significant contributions of responsive regulation approach to the regulatory literature, asserted that responsive regulation contain some limitations that may limit the applicability of the approach (Harvard Law Review 1993; Mendeloff 1993; Scholz 1993).

This book, like the study by Scholz (1984), however, believes that suggesting an optimal strategy is appropriate. This is why the middle course approach is proposed as a strategy to fill in the gap between the *"sterile context between deregulation and stronger regulation"* (Ayres & Braithwaite 1992 p. 101). The contribution of the middle course approach can, therefore, be seen in the light of the limitation of these two proposals. Voluntary compliance is concerned with the efficiency of enforcement, while responsive regulation is concerned with effectiveness of enforcement represented by the desire to avoid capture since *"they devote little attention to the likelihood that applying standards will require more agency resources than applying rules"* (Harvard Law Review 1993 p. 1688).

Socio-economic Theory of Regulatory Compliance

Like all theories of regulation, Sutinen and Kuperan (1999) theory of compliance seeks to find a better way to improve compliance, but unlike the self-protecting theory, the focus is mainly on the efficiency of compliance rather than both the effectiveness of regulation and efficiency of compliance. This distinction is discussed in the next chapter on the contribution of the self-protecting theory but what distinguished self-protecting from other theories mentioned in this book is the desire to look at the problem from both the perspective of regulators who want more effectiveness and the desire of the regulated who want more efficiency. The assumption implicit in Sutinen and Kuperan (1999) argument is that efficient compliance implies effective regulation. However, as discussed by Ayres and Braithwaite (1992), efficiency of compliance may lead to capture which hampers effectiveness of regulation.

In addition, Sutinen and Kuperan (1999) is concerned more with individual behaviour rather than organisational behaviour, while the self-protecting theory deals with both individual and organisational behaviour since the theory itself explains individual behaviour while the framework dereived from the theory explains organisational behaviour. Sutinen and Kuperan (1999) theory is, however, in line with the self-protecting theory in that deterrence alone is insufficient to explain regulatory and compliance behaviour. The intrinsic and extrinsic motivation introduced by Sutinen and Kuperan (1999) is also in line with the concepts of culture, ethics, conviction and belief presented in this book.

Context of AML

Although AML is about regulation and compliance, it is however important to mention that it is unlike other regulatory environments. In Becker (1968) and Tyler (2006), for example, the focus is on individuals, while Stigler (1971), Scholz (1984) and Ayres and Braithwaite (1992) focus on the behaviour of firms. In AML, however, the ultimate targets are not the regulated firms, but money launderers who use the firms' system to launder proceeds of crime. In AML, therefore, firms are acting as agent of regulators to prevent criminal behaviour (Araujo 2008). As a result of this, the normal strategy for enforcement, though applicable, are not necessarily well suited for AML (Takats 2011). Furthermore, although AML aligns with the public interest view of regulation since the ultimate aim is to prevent money laundering, which is believed to have detrimental effect on the economy and on the welfare of citizens, it seems that is not viewed as such by the public in whose name the fight is being waged (Harvey & Lau 2009).

Despite this difference in context between other regulations and AML, however, the theories of regulations mentioned earlier are still applicable because the essential ingredients of capture (Ayres & Braithwaite 1992), cost of compliance (Masciandaro 1999), conflict of interest (Scholz 1984) are present in all regulatory behaviour.

Conclusion

The issue of regulation has been around for ages. It is about the desire of public agencies to exert control over companies and individuals. The reason why there is regulation is, therefore, mainly to check market excesses and to protect the right of individuals and the society.

There is, however, a debate on the best way of regulation. Some prefer more regulation while others prefer less regulation, and it is this argument that is at the heart of the regulation and deregulation debate. There is also the argument of which approach is better. The economists argue that economic theories are enough to explain the basis for regulation while social theorist argued that economic theories are insufficient to explain compliance with regulation. The efficiency and effectiveness consideration is, however, a more interesting argument because the proponents of regulation and deregulation as well as the economic and social theorist are all interested in the effectiveness and efficiency of regulation. It is for this reason that this chapter focuses on the trade-off between the two concepts. The self-protecting theory's contribution to the debate is that it explains this trade-off and provides a recommendation for an effective and efficient regulation and compliance. It also bridges the gap between the economic and social theories by providing a middle course approach.

In summary, the literature on regulation was reviewed since the self-protecting theory is essentially a theory of regulation. The old age debate between regulation and deregulation, which is all about the effectiveness and efficiency consideration was highlighted to show how the self-protecting theory fits into the debate. The theory is also a social as well as an economic theory. This was discussed in the chapter, but more importantly, it was shown that the theory is a combination of the two contending theories. In the next chapter, a more detailed discussion is presented to show how the self-protecting theory can potentially help to solve the regulatory problem discussed in this chapter.

5

The Potential Solution to the Dilemma

Introduction

The *self-protecting* theory is essentially a theory of regulation. It explains how MLROs balance the desire of regulators to have an effective regulation and the desire of banks to have an efficient compliance. The chapter presents the Middle-Course Approach, a potential solution to the effectiveness and efficiency trade-off. The approach was discovered from the *self-protecting* framework which suggests that for an effective and efficient AML regulation and compliance, MLROs should be treated fairly and given the required independence to perform their function of implementing AML regulations. Unlike the research by Scholz (1984) and Ayres and Braithwaite (1992) that attributed the problem of compliance to toughness of regulation and capture respectively, which are all looking at the problem of regulation from the perspective of enforcement, the middle-course approach is looking at the problem from the point of the regulated. This is similar to the study by Tyler (2006), but unlike Tyler (2006) and Becker (1968) that looked at criminal

A.U. Bello, *Improving Anti-Money Laundering Compliance*,
Palgrave Studies in Risk, Crime and Society,
DOI 10.1007/978-3-319-43264-9_5

behaviour, middle-course approach is looking at those charged with ensuring the prevention of criminal behaviour. As stated earlier, the target of AML is not banks or MLROs but money launderers; banks and MLROs are agents of the regulators responsible for preventing money launderers from using the banking system to commit money laundering offences (Araujo 2008).

Public and Private Interest Theory

Before presenting the middle-course approach, it is important to explain briefly the public and private interest theories, which are at the heart of the trade-off between effectiveness and efficiency. The public interest theory is more related to the concept of effectiveness of enforcement while the private interest theory is more related to efficiency of compliance (Dolar & Shughart II 2011).

The distinction between private and public interest theories was captured well by Kroszner and Strahan (1999 p. 1437) when they stated that private interest theory of regulation is the process *"in which well-organised groups use the coerce power of state to capture rent at the expense of the more disperse group"* while public interest is the process *"in which government intervention correct market failure and maximise social welfare"*.

According to Dolar and Shughart II (2011), Stigler (1971) was the first economist to make a formal contribution to the private interest theory, although the theory has been in existence in the sociology field long before Stigler made his contribution (Bentley 1967; Truman 1971). In "*The Theory of Economic Regulation*", it was stated that stated that *"as a rule, regulation is acquired by the industry and is designed and operated primarily for its benefit"* Stigler (1971 p. 3) contrary to the widely held belief that regulation is established for the benefit of the public (Laffont & Tirole 1991).

Relating the public and private interest theories to the effectiveness and efficiency trade-off, the concern in public theory is more to do with effectiveness; *"possibly owing to its normative nature, the public interest theory focuses on the benefits of regulation and downplays its social costs or 'unintended' consequences"* (Dolar & Shughart II 2011 p. 21) while the private interest theory is concerned with how firms are maximising *"the well-being of their members rather than that of the public at large"* (Dolar & Shughart II 2011 p. 21). This implies that firms, based on the private interest theory, are more concerned with efficient use of compliance resources.

What emanates from this discussion is the relationship between enforcement and effectiveness, on the one hand, and compliance and efficiency, on the other hand. The point being made is that enforcement is the preserve of the regulators, and their main aim is to make it effective, while compliance is for the regulated, and their main aim is to make it efficient. This is similar to the deterrence versus compliance model of regulation discussed in Ayres and Braithwaite (1992) in which some believe that sanction is the best in enforcing the law (deterrence) and other who believe persuasion is better (compliance).

This book, therefore, builds on this notion but looks at it from a holistic view, since much of the research in this field is centred around the deterrence model (Ayres & Braithwaite 1992). The issue of effectiveness and efficiency would therefore be analysed from the point of view of regulators as well as from the point of view of the regulated. That is what is effective and efficient for the regulators and what is effective and efficient for the regulated sector rather that looking at effectiveness from the point of view of regulators and efficiency from the point of view of regulated as in Scholz (1984), Ayres and Braithwaite (1992) and Masciandaro (1999).

This book also attempts to situate the various debates within the self-protecting framework. Voluntary compliance approach of Scholz (1984), for example, relates to *cooperating* which implies *self-regulation*, while Becker (1968) approach relates to the *communicating* quadrant representing *tough regulation*. Tyler (2006) is also situated in the *cooperating* quadrant (*self-regulation*) because of its emphasis on legitimacy as a means of obeying the law. Ayres and Braithwaite (1992) on the other hand are scattered across the framework since they do not have a single optimal strategy for all circumstances. Republican tripartism and partial industry intervention, for example, are closer to *smart regulation*, while enforced self-regulation belongs to the *self-regulation* quadrant. Similarly, the Tit for Tat approach (Axelrod 1980; Scholz 1984) can also be placed within the framework as will be seen later in the chapter.

Summary of the Self-protecting Theory

Before presenting the middle-course approach, it is important to discuss the various strategies implied in the self-protecting theory in the light of the other theories reviewed in this chapter. The strategies will be discussed by the use of the following self-protecting framework (Fig. 5.1).

Discharging

As discussed in Chap. 3, MLROs are *discharging* their responsibility to protect themselves rather than *complying* with regulation when they are *aligning* with banks and are under *unfair pressure* from regulators. The

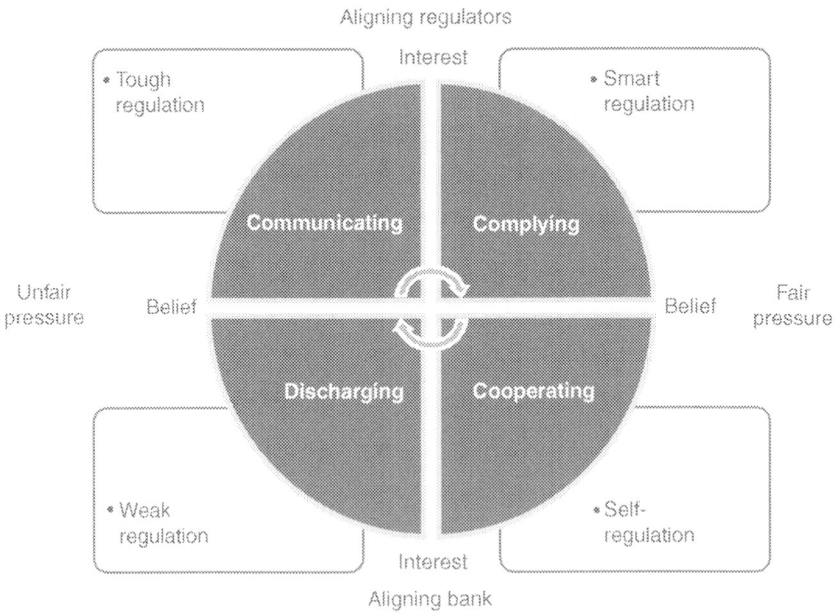

Fig. 5.1 Self-protecting framework

regulatory regime that results from this behaviour is *weak regulation* since MLROs are just doing enough (*discharging*) to avoid sanction, punishment and damage to their reputation (Favarel-Garrigues et al., 2008). A statement of one MLRO best illustrates this behaviour; "*the only reason why banks are fighting money laundering is because, under the law, they are required to fight it otherwise there is no point commercially to do that*".

Likewise, in the model by Scholz (1984), this behaviour is similar to temptation where firms evade when regulators are cooperating and in so doing they benefit from their compliance strategy at the expense of the effectiveness of enforcing regulation since, according to Axelrod (1980 p. 4), " *if one defects while the other cooperates, the defecting side gets the highest payoff*". The defecting side, in this case, are the banks while the cooperating side are the regulators.

Communicating

The *communicating* behaviour is also similar to the harassment quadrant of Scholz (1984) in that they *align* with regulators to comply with regulation not necessarily because they believe in the system but because their self-interest may be threatened by the regulators through sanction, fine and reputation damage (Favarel-Garrigues et al., 2008). As one MLRO stated; "*my concern is to make sure that I discharge my responsibility to the authorities because I don't want to be a victim*".

They also *communicate* within the banks to protect themselves against the banks rather that *cooperate* with the banks to protect the interest of the banks. The same MLRO was willing to use *threat*, a property of *communicating*, by saying that "*if I want to do my job and my director is not allowing me to do it, I will send a memo to him about my concerns. When the [name of authority] ask me why I did not do what I am expected to do, I will show them the memo; that way I am covered.*"

The regulation that results from this behaviour, according to the self-protecting framework, is called *tough regulation*. In this situation, like the harassment quadrant of Scholz (1984), regulators are benefiting from the arrangement by using the deterrence approach even when ultimately it may be at the expense of the banks. This again agrees with the statement *"if one defects while the other cooperates, the defecting side gets the highest payoff"* (Axelrod 1980 p. 4). In this case, the defecting side are the regulators while the cooperating side are the banks.

Complying

Similarly, MLROs that are under fair pressure and aligning with regulators are complying with regulation rather that discharging to protect themselves. This is best illustrated by the saying of one MLRO who stated that "*I would not blame the regulators for putting pressure on us because that is the only way to ensure compliance."* The regulatory regime that results from this behaviour is *smart regulation.* This quadrant represents the divergence between the Scholz (1984) and the self-protecting framework. While Scholz (1984) called it confrontation or legalistic battle, the self-protecting framework calls it *smart regulation.* It also different from the prisoners dilemma's approach of Axelrod (1980 p. 4), *"if both do defect, both do poorly"*.

Cooperating

In the same way, the MLROs under fair pressure and who align with banks are cooperating to prevent money laundering. An example from the data is when one MLRO stated that, *"It is true that there can be a conflict between banks and regulators with an MLRO in the middle but I don't have that problem because I have all the support I need from the bank."*

This behaviour fits the voluntary compliance quadrant of Scholz (1984) since both parties are maximising their benefit without minimising the benefit of the other that is if *"both cooperate, both do fairly well"* (Axelrod 1980 p. 4). The research called this behaviour *cooperating*, and the strategy coming out of it, *self-regulation.* It represents the ideal situation, according to Scholz (1984), but only if banks subordinate their interest to the interest of regulators. That the banks may not subordinate their interest is the fear expressed by Ayres and Braithwaite (1992) that will make the strategy ineffective.

The relationship between these two models as relates to effectiveness and efficiency may be apparent based on the above analysis. The assumption inherent in the above discussion is that the interest of the two parties conflict that is the concern of regulators is to maximise pollution reduction (effectiveness) and the concern of banks is to minimise compliance cost (efficiency). Relating this to AML compliance based on the assumption that the concern of regulators is to prevent money laundering and the concern of banks is to maximise shareholder wealth, discharging is more efficient for the bank but less effective the regulators. On the other hand, communicating is more effective to the regulators but less efficient for the bank. Similarly, complying is less efficient for bank and less effective for the regulators but it is better than discharging for the regulators and communicating for the bank. The best option among the four self-protecting strategies is therefore cooperating which is similar to voluntary compliance in the model by Scholz (1984).

The Middle-course Approach—The Fifth Strategy

How much does it cost the AML regulators to prevent money laundering? And what is the benefit to banks in spending money on complying with AML regulation? This is the other side of the effectiveness and efficiency debate that is largely ignored in the literature. The middle-course approach is, therefore, an attempt to address this gap by finding an approach that considers effectiveness and efficiency from the perspective of both the regulated and the regulators.

It is important to point out that the middle-course approach emerged as a better approach to compliance from the self-protecting framework, which further confirms the workability of the theory, its relevance and its fitness. The process of emergence will be demonstrated as follows:

Figure 5.2 shows the framework from both the perspective of banks and regulators, but from the point of view of MLROs. By breaking down the figure further into a high and low quadrant, the perspective of each party will become apparent as shown below (Figs. 5.3 and 5.4).

From Fig. 5.3 and 5.4, it is clear that the two perspectives are different. High fairness and high alignment is *complying* from the perspective of

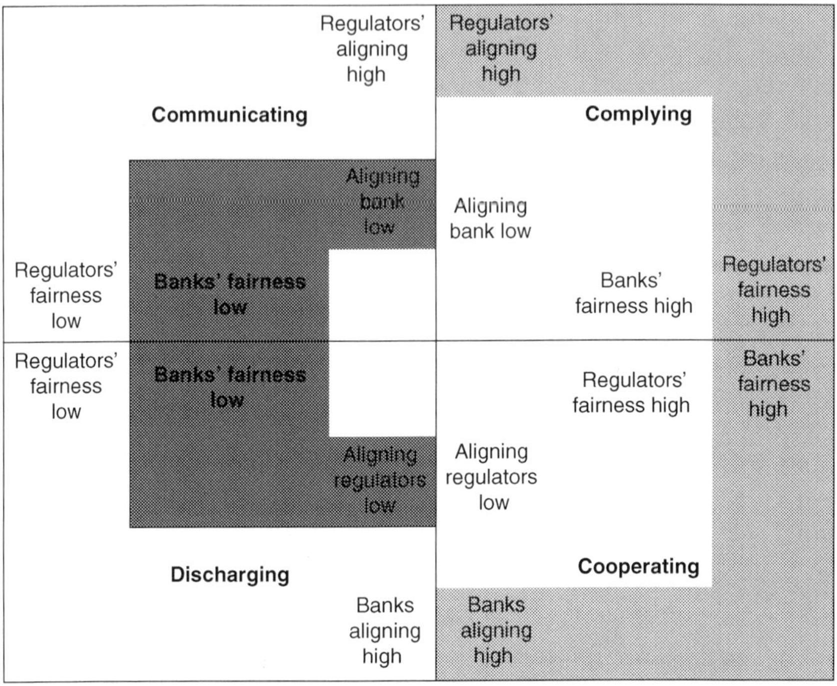

Fig. 5.2 Emergence of the middle-course approach

regulators but *cooperating* from the perspective of banks. Similarly, the other quadrants are also different as would be explained in the following section.

From the Perspective of the Regulators

Communicating

When aligning with regulators is high and fair pressure from the regulator is low, the behaviour is called *communicating* which means the MLROs are just conforming to regulations not necessarily because they believe in them but because of the threat of prosecution and imposition of high penalties by the regulators. This is called *tough regulation*. This may be effective for the

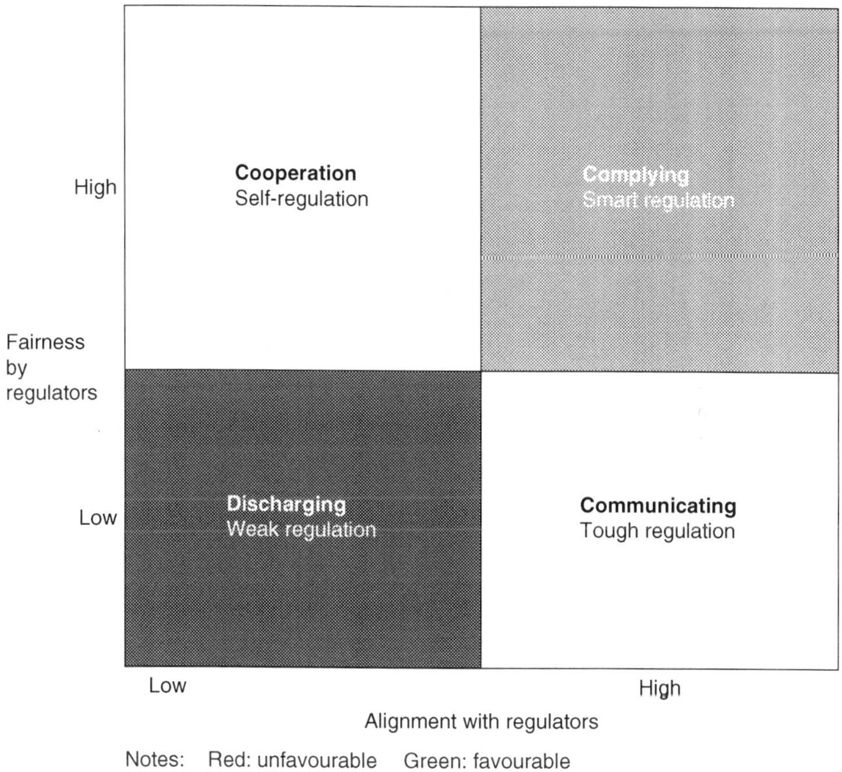

Fig. 5.3 Regulators' perspective

regulators but not necessarily efficient because toughness (or deterrence) approach is inherently costly (Sutinen & Kuperan 1999) for regulators.

Complying

If, however, fairness on the part of regulators is high and *aligning* of MLROs with the regulators is high, then the MLROs are *complying* with regulation, which is good for regulators, and the strategy is called *smart regulation*. This strategy may be more effective since MLROs are *complying* with regulations, and can also be relatively efficient because the fairness from the regulators will make them more legitimate, and this

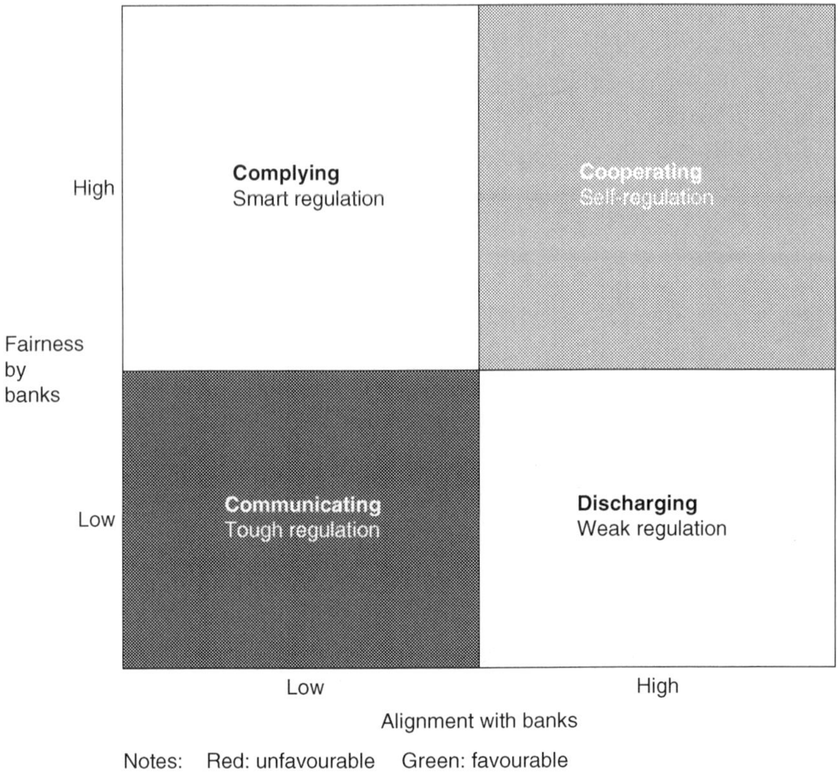

Fig. 5.4 Banks' perspective

will in turn make banks to be willing to incur compliance cost to obey a legitimate authority (Tyler 2006). It is relatively efficient because the regulators still have to bear much of the cost of compliance.

Cooperating

The same applies to high fairness but low aligning giving *cooperation* (*self-regulation*) which may be more efficient for regulators since it is banks that would shoulder most of the responsibilities, but it is not necessarily effective because of the potential for capture i.e. influencing regulation for their own benefit (Ayres & Braithwaite 1992).

Discharging

The worst MLRO behaviour from the perspective of regulators is, however, *discharging*. This is the situation where there is low fairness from the regulators and low aligning of MLROs with the regulators. This produces *weak regulation* (in red) which is ineffective for the regulators as discussed in Chap. 3. This is mainly because MLROs, and invariably the banks, are just *discharging* their responsibility to protect themselves rather than *complying* with regulation to prevent money laundering. The strategy is also inefficient for the regulators because of the increased cost of enforcement that would be necessary to make them comply.

From the Perspective of the Bank

Discharging

When *aligning* with banks is high and fair pressure from the banks is low (unfair pressure), The behaviour is called *discharging* which means MLROs are just *discharging* their responsibilities but not necessarily *complying* with regulations, and this is called *weak regulation*. This may be more effective for the bank in maximising profit from potential suspicious activities, but may not be efficient in the long run because of the potential cost of pressure on MLRO since agencies are advised to be *"unrelenting in pursuit of chronic evaders"* (Scholz 1984 p. 385). The case of Coutts & Company fined £8.75 million for weaknesses in AML control is an example how effective it can be for a bank to increase profitability in the short term, but eventually inefficient because of the cost of an enforcement action. (Financial Conduct Authority 2013a). A participant even mentioned this in one of the interviews when he said that banks tend to forget that the cost of enforcement action is much more than the fines imposed by the regulators. He stated that

> If you consider the cost of rectifying the mistakes after [name of agency]'s enforcement action then you will see what I mean. I was talking to a friend who was an MLRO in one of the banks that was sanctioned by

[name of agency]. He said although the fine of £1.6 million may be small, the cost of implementing additional systems and controls, employing staff, dealing with backlogs of suspicious activity transactions and responding to [name of agency] was enormous. He told me that, eventually, the total cost was within the region of £20 million.

Cooperating

If, however, fairness on the part of banks is high and *aligning* of MLROs with banks is also high then MLROs are *cooperating* to prevent money laundering, and this is called *self-regulation*. This may be more effective for the banks, since they have control over the regulatory process and the threat of heavy penalty that would reduce profits is low. Again this is similar to the Tit for Tat approach that requires *"agencies to be reasonable towards cooperative firms"* (Scholz 1984 p. 385). Example of a situation where a regulator was lenient was the case of Turkish Bank where the FSA reduced an imposed penalty of £420,000 when the bank cooperated with the investigation (Financial Service Authority 2012). This strategy can however only be relatively efficient since banks have to bear much of the cost of regulation (Zimiles 2004).

Complying

The same applies for high fairness by banks but low *aligning* of MLROs with the banks giving *smart regulation*. This may be more efficiency for banks since it is the regulators that are mostly responsible for the cost of enforcement, but it can be relative ineffective since a fair pressure is not necessarily a soft pressure. Pressure can be fair from the perspective of the MLRO and the bank but may result in excessive cost of compliance that would reduce the profit of the bank. The Deepwater Horizon oil spill incident is an example of how regulation may be considered fair but excessive (Cleveland et al. 2010). It might have been fair to ask BP to clean up the problem that was caused by the oil spill but, in doing so, BP would have incurred high costs that would have negatively affected their profitability. The case of EFG Private Bank that was fined £4.2 m for breach of AML regulations (Financial Conduct Authority 2013a) may also be another example.

Communicating

Similarly, the worst MLRO behaviour from the perspective of banks is *communicating* which implies *tough regulation*. In this situation, the pressure on MLRO mainly from banks is unfair and aligning with the banks is also low. It is not effective for the banks because a tough action may necessitate increased cost of compliance as the expense of profitability. In the UK, for example, the AML regime, according to Ryder (2008) is not cost effective as the compliance cost has increased significantly since its introduction.

It is equally inefficient since more resources would be expended to ensure compliance. Again it is inefficient based on the suggestion by Scholz (1984) that advise agencies to be *"vengeful towards cheaters"*. There are several examples in the literature supporting the stance of regulators towards "*cheaters*". Examples of such enforcement action on UK banks include the penalty of $298 million and $350 million imposed on Barclays and Lloyds bank respectively in the US for illegal transactions relating to the US sanction regime (New York District Attorney 2012).

In summary, complying is good for banks and self-regulation is good for regulators but only in an ideal situation. And this is at the heart of the debate about effectiveness and efficiency. Regulators may prefer self-regulation because the strategy will be more efficient for them, but they cannot be certain that it will be effective since obeying regulation is at the mercy of the banks who can decide not to enforce it. This may result in banks going from *cooperating* to *discharging* or in Scholz (1984)'s model from cooperating to evading. On the other hand, smart regulation may be more efficient for banks since the cost is mostly borne by the regulators, but they cannot be certain that regulators will keep to their word to behave fairly. This may result in regulators going from *smart regulation* to *tough regulation* or in Scholz's (1984) model from cooperation to deterrence.

It is clear for the above that the self-regulation (called voluntary compliance) suggested by Scholz (1984) as a good approach for enforcement is fraught with challenges that Ayres and Braithwaite (1992) correctly identified as the potential for capture. If, however, efficiency and not effectiveness is the goal of enforcement and effectiveness and not efficiency is the goal of compliance, then *self-regulation* may be a better approach for regulators and banks respectively. If, however, effectiveness and not efficiency is the goal of enforcement and efficiency and not effectiveness is the goal of compliance, then *smart regulation* may be a better approach for regulators and banks respectively. To have a regulation that is both effective and efficient for regulators and banks, a middle-course approach is required that would combine part of *self-regulation* with part of *smart regulation*, and this is the approach that is proposed in this study.

Emergence of the Middle-course Approach

The emergence of the middle-course approach as a potential solution to the trade-off is best illustrated by the following diagram and the analysis that follows (Fig. 5.5).

The middle course is a mid-way between *smart regulation* and *self-protecting* that is, combining the best of *smart regulation* with the best of *self-regulation*. From Fig. 5.5 above, a low *aligning* with banks (AB-low) and a high fair pressure (FB-high) from the banks is *complying* or *smart regulation*, and a low *aligning* with regulators (AR-low) and a high fair pressure from the regulators (FR-high) is *cooperation* or *self-regulating*.

It was shown earlier that a *smart regulation* is effective for the regulators but less efficient while self-regulation is effective for the banks, but less efficient. Combining the two approaches may, therefore, produce a middle course that is effective and relatively more efficient for both the banks and the regulators. This is because at the extreme end of *self-regulation* the potential for capture will be high, and therefore ineffective for the regulators but effective for the banks, and at the extreme end of smart regulation the cost of enforcement would be high and therefore inefficient for the

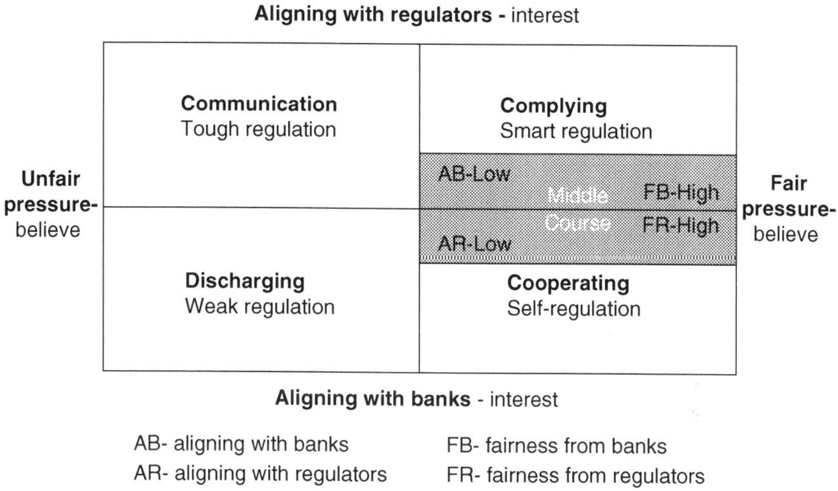

Fig. 5.5 The middle-course approach

regulators, but efficient for banks. Hence the middle-course approach has provided a possible solution to the problem of capture (Ayres & Braithwaite 1992) associated with cooperating by having a more efficient cooperation, and the problem of increased cost of enforcement (Scholz 1984) associated with complying by having a more efficient compliance for the banks.

An important characteristic of the middle-course region seen in the diagram above is that MLROs have low alignment with both the regulators and the banks (represented by AR-low and AB-low). This, in essence, means that MLROs (or compliance officers) are relatively independent since they are neither aligned with banks at the expense of regulators nor are the aligned with regulators at the expense of banks. This idea of independence is similar to the republican tripartism proposal of Ayres and Braithwaite (1992) which suggests engaging a public interest group to be part of the enforcement process. In this approach, however, the MLROs form part of the tripod instead of an external party that may not be cost effective. It is this cost implication of involving an external third party that is part of the criticism of the republican tripartism (Harvard Law Review 1993; Mendeloff 1993; Scholz 1993).

Who is going to train the public interest groups (PIGs)? Who is going to resource them? And at what cost should they be introduced? These are some of the question asked by the researchers.

The idea of the independence of the MLROs may even be what one participant suggested when he said that, *"one solution that may help is for regulators and banks to share the burden of paying the salaries of MLROs"*. The middle-course approach can also solve the problem associated with training and funding since MLROs are well experienced, capable and willing as discovered in the study underpinning this book and the suggestion by Bosworth-Davies (1998) and Webb (2004). There is also not going to be a fundamental change to the existing structure by adopting the approach since compliance departments are currently well established (KPMG 2011). What is required for the approach to work however is for both regulators and banks to provide fair pressure with a reasonable level of independence that a fair pressure would demand.

One of the ways that may ensure fair pressure is for *reward* and *punishment* to be fair. Fair *reward* and *punishment* means *punishment* should be commensurate with the offence while *reward* should take into consideration the risk to MLROs for working to expose money launderers. MLROs should also be treated as equals in the regulators process as suggested Ayres and Braithwaite (1992) as one of the conditions for PIGs participation. They should also be part of the intelligence sharing community according to one participant instead of threatening them with prosecution, which *"does not make sense"*, said another. Further research in this area may however reveal better ways of ensuring fair pressure on MLROs.

The middle-course approach is, therefore, predicated on treating MLROs fairly. Although the role of fairness in regulation has been studied by researchers as seen in Sutinen and Kuperan (1999) and Tyler (2006), this approach has tried to show how fairness can be achieved by providing a theoretical framework for determining it. This framework is the self-protecting framework which has *complaining*, *belief* and *interest* as the concepts that determine what is fair.

Another issue is that fair is relative; what one considered fair may not be fair to another. The question then is what is and what is not a legitimate concern? The middle-course approach addresses this by trying to identify where banks and regulators agree with each as regards what are legitimate concerns. This may be done by interviewing both parties to find out areas of common concern. An example of this from the data may be appropriate. The implementation of the consent regimes, for example, is one of the main concerns of MLROs. It was, however, discovered during a chanced interview with a senior law enforcement officer that he also believes the consent regime is faulty. Consent may, therefore, be a common concern. A possible solution to the problem may, therefore, be to amend the provision to ensure fair pressure on MLROs and more efficient enforcement of the AML regulation.

Conclusion

Finding a solution to the regulation and deregulation debate has been the preoccupation of many scholars in various disciplines. To regulate, or not to regulate? This has been the main question engaging the minds of public officers. Some have imposed more regulation to protect the rights of individuals and to correct market failures while others have preferred less regulation. That the question has remained unanswered suggests that a balance needs to be found that would address this problem, which is essentially an issue of the trade-off between efficiency and effectiveness. This is best explained by the public and private interest theories where concern over effectiveness is at the centre of the public theory while concern over efficiency is the centre of the private interest theory.

The middle-course approach recommended in this chapter is, therefore, an attempt to address the regulatory problem, at least in the AML environment. The approach was derived from the self-protecting theory which states that the more there is unfair pressures on compliance officers the more they protects themselves rather than assist in regulation.

Furthermore, the approach was developed through a rigorous process of theory building. Independence and fairness emerged as the two key concepts that are needed for an effective an efficient AML system. A compliance officer that has the required level of independence and is treated fairly, for example, is more likely to assist in regulation than an officer who is treated unfairly and lacks the necessary freedom to exercise his judgement.

It is, however, important to remember that grounded theory is not findings, but a plausible set of hypotheses that explain a substantive area. Although a grounded theory is only an integrated set of hypotheses, *"these hypotheses, which become treated as findings, are often enough for its users"* (Glaser 1998 p. 3). Accordingly, the middle course approach should be seen in this light, which means that it is modifiable, as with all grounded theories, based on further constant comparison.

In summary, this chapter provides a potential solution to the regulatory dilemma by presenting the middle-course approach as a better approach to regulation and compliance at least in the AML environment. The approach, which was derived from the self-protecting theory, contends that a better approach is to find a middle ground between the various theories on regulation and compliance. These theories were reviewed to show the similarities and difference between them and the self-protecting theory. In the end, the middle-course approach was presented as a compromise between the two main contending theories, but with the potential of addressing the effectiveness and efficiency trade-off.

6

General Application of the Self-protecting Theory

Introduction

Although it is evident that the contribution of the self-protecting theory has been established because a theory was discovered to explain the protecting behaviour of MLROs and a recommendation was provided for an effective and efficient AML, it is, however, important to make the contribution more explicit by relating the theory to other substantive areas where it could be applicable.

Following the advice of Urquhart (2013), the contribution is illustrated using Walsham's analytical generalisation framework (Walsham 1995) in which a theoretical contribution is illustrated using four ways namely: development of concepts, generation of theory, drawing specific implication and contributing to rich insights.

A.U. Bello, *Improving Anti-Money Laundering Compliance,*
Palgrave Studies in Risk, Crime and Society,
DOI 10.1007/978-3-319-43264-9_6

Development of Concepts

To highlight the contribution of the *self-protecting* theory in this regard, three concepts will be presented as illustrations to show their contribution to knowledge, that is, *unfair pressure, marginal management* and *shifting expectation*. Before discussing these properties, it is important to acknowledge other concepts discovered in this research that are related to pre-existing concepts in the literature to show their similarities and difference as follows.

Organisational Culture

Culture is a well-established concept in the literature, from a concept more general that includes *"something some people were doing, or exhorted others to do"* (Bauman 2003 p. 8) to a more specific type that deals with organisational culture, which is related to the concept of *culture* discovered in this research.

Culture, in general, deals with the way of life of people in different locations and environments (Markus & Kitayama 1991). It covers their belief, their history and the guiding principle behind their behaviours. Organisational culture, on the other hand, is a subset of culture and according to Edgar H Schein (2004 p. 14) it:

> is the pattern of basic assumptions that a given group has invented, discovered, or developed in learning to cope with its problems of external adaptation and internal integration—a pattern of assumptions that has worked well enough to be considered valid and, therefore, to be taught to new members as the correct way to perceive, think, and feel in relation to those problems.

There are, however, different definitions of organisational culture (Cooke & Rousseau 1988) but in essence it is the *"shared beliefs and values guiding the thinking and behavioural styles of members"* (Cooke & Rousseau 1988 p. 245).

In the light of the focus of this book, which is about anti-money laundering (AML) within the banking industry, organisational culture is more relevant to the discussion of the concept of *culture* generated in this research.

Organisational culture can be viewed from two different perspectives. There is the academic view that considered the whole organisation as a culture and there is the practitioners' view that considered culture as a way of enhancing the effectiveness of an organisation (Barley et al. 1988). This research is aligned more with the practitioners' view of a strong and a weak culture made popular by authors such as Ouchi and Price (1978), Deal and Kennedy (1988) and Peters and Waterman (2006). Much of what is written on organisational culture from this perspective suggests that a strong culture implies excellent performance (Denison 1990; Denison & Mishra 1995; Kono & Clegg 1998). Denison and Mishra (1995) for example showed that culture has a positive effect on performance. Kono and Clegg (1998 p. 22) also found that *"companies with vitalized cultures have higher financial performance that companies without such culture"*. There are, however, some studies that disagreed with this view (Kotter 2008; Saffold 1988). While Saffold (1988) argued that the *"strong culture hypothesis"* is flawed, Kotter (2008) found that leadership rather than a strong culture is more important is correcting an unhealthy culture. He even stated that *"it seems firms can have a strong culture, but poor performance and a weak culture, but excellent performance"* (Kotter 2008 p. 21). The role of leadership in organisational culture is shared by E. H. Schein (2010 p. 1) who stated that there is *"intimate relationship between culture and leadership"*.

Whatever the difference between the two sides, what is evident and agreed upon by all is that some organisations can be said to have a strong culture while others can have a weak culture (Deal & Kennedy 1988; Denison 1990; Kotter 2008; Saffold 1988), which is consistent with the findings in this book. What is different, however, is that the focus in this book is on the link between culture and behaviour of individuals. The importance of the link between culture and behaviour was highlighted in Harvey and Bosworth-Davies (2013) showing how the changing culture in the UK financial markets is affecting the behaviour of participants in the market.

The literature that deals with culture and control is, however, more aligned with this book, since the focus is to determine how the culture in an organisation affects the decision of MLROs to align with their banks or with regulators. Kunda (2009), indicates that there are at least two relationships between culture and control; the traditional view that is based on the utilitarian form of control and the contemporary view that is based on a normative view of control. In the traditional view, it is about controlling employees by reward and punishment while in the contemporary view, employees willingly accept to be controlled because they believe in the organisation.

It is this normative view that relates to the concept of culture discussed in this book. However, rather than looking at culture from the point of view of control (in relation to adhering to the rules and regulations of an organisation), this book is looking at culture from the relationship between an organisation (bank) and a third party (regulator). This distinction is important because an organisation might have a set of rules that they want to enforce, but it may conflict with a different set of rules that a regulator wants to enforce. How are MLROs going to behave? Are they going to align with their banks or are they going to align with regulators?

In the case where there is a conflict, other variables such as the personal ethics of MLROs comes into play to guide them in their decision making (see the section on ethics later in the chapter). If, however, there is no conflict between the objectives of the bank and the objective of the regulators then there is little pressure on an MLRO. This is based on the premise that the objectives of regulators align with a strong culture since regulators *"are viewed as benevolent maximizers of social welfare"* (Laffont & Tirole 1991 p. 1089). Therefore, the finding in this book is that a bank that supports compliance is regarded as having a strong culture, while a bank that does not is regarded as having a weak culture.

A strong culture in this book, therefore, means that a bank is also concerned with preventing money laundering, while a weak culture is the culture in a bank that is not interested in preventing money laundering, but rather it is more interested in making a profit. The finding in this book suggests MLROs that are working in banks that have a strong culture have less pressure in complying with their AML responsibilities than those working in organisations that have a weak culture.

Belief

Another concept discovered is belief, which is also well established in the literature. According to Fishbein and Ajzen (1975 p. 131), *"beliefs refer to a person's subjective probability judgement concerning some discriminable aspect of his world; they deal with person's understanding of himself and his environment"*.

The concept of belief in this book is less technical than the above definition but more in line with the definition of *Crow and Liggett* (2014 *p. 1532) that "beliefs are a conviction of the truth of something"* and has as its main sources; social, culture, experience and environment. This definition is in line with the concept of belief in this book that has three properties, that is, *conviction, ethics* and *culture.*

Thus, the link between ethics and beliefs, for example, has been highlighted by researchers including Blasi (1980 p. 2) who stated that *"moral action has been viewed either as the immediate result of action tendencies and of their interplay or as mediated by such cognitive processes as moral definitions, moral beliefs, and moral reasoning"*. This is also the conclusion of Sayre-McCord (2012 p. 56) who state that by *"a person's moral beliefs are epistemically justified if, and then to the extent that, they cohere well with the other things she believes"*.

As for the relationship between culture and belief, this is evident from the definition of culture found in the literature. In some of the definitions, the place of belief as a determinant of culture is well established. For example it has been defined as the *"shared beliefs and values guiding the thinking and behavioural styles of members"* (Cooke & Rousseau 1988 p. 245) and *"the shared patterns of thought, belief, feelings and values"* E.H. Schein (2010 p. 73). Similarly, Denison (1990 p. 94) described the culture of a company as its *"ideology and belief system"*.

Belief as used in this book is, therefore, a concept that encompasses *ethics, culture* and *convictions,* the three properties of belief generated from the research behind this book.

Ethics

Although the focus of this book is on personal ethics and its effect in influencing the behaviour of an MLRO, it is important to give a description of ethics, which has been a topic of considerable discussion for centuries (Kraut 1994). This section provides a brief overview of three major ethical theories of deontology, utilitarianism and virtue ethics (Solomon 1992). The theories are relevant in understanding behaviours in organisations (Dion 2012), and they are presented to see to what extent their concept of moral reasoning could be related to the concept of *ethics* presented in this book.

Deontology

Deontology is an ethical theory made famous by Immanuel Kant, which in its basic form rejects the idea that the end justifies the means, but rather the means itself has to be justified (Shafer-Landau 2007). It is based on the premise that a person ought to perform a certain action not because it will serve his interest or bring him happiness, but because it is the right thing to do. For example, lying is morally wrong while speaking the truth is right, and this is true independent of the consequences of each action. This view is succinctly put by Kant (1964 p. 21).

> A good will is not good because of what it effects or accomplishes, because of its fitness to attain some proposed end, but only because of its volition, that is, it is good in itself and, regarded for itself, is to be valued incomparably higher than all that could merely be brought about by it in favor of some inclination and indeed, if you will, of the sum of all inclinations.

In deontological ethics, therefore, a person should *"act only in accordance with that maxim through which you can at the same time will that it become a universal law"* (Kant 1964 p. 37).

Utilitarianism

Utilitarianism, on the other hand, is the view that the focus should be towards maximising pleasure or happiness. The founder of the theory is Jeremy Bentham (Singer 1974), who holds that the desire for pleasure should determine an action and that all pleasures are equal. This view is captured by the following *"the game of push-pin is of equal value with the arts and sciences of music and poetry"* (Bentham 1825 p. 206). Mill (1870), however, while being true to the idea of utilitarianism, holds that some pleasures are higher than others.

Using our example above, a person that holds the utilitarian view will lie if the outcome would produce happiness or pleasure or as stated by Mill (1870 p. 9) *"actions are right in proportion as they tend to promote happiness, wrong as they tend to produce the reverse of happiness"*.

Virtue Ethics

As for virtue ethics, it received renewed interest in recent centuries, mostly inspired by the moral philosophy of Aristotle (Slote 1995). The foundation of the philosophy is that it places the virtue of character above rules and consequences (Hursthouse 1999; Reeve 2014). According to Aristotle, an act is a virtuous act if it is the act of a virtuous individual (Aristoteles 1893). Such individual traits include truthfulness, honesty and courage among others. There is, however a contemporary view that seeks to align virtue theory to relativism, but this is held by Nussbaum (1988) to be contrary to virtue ethics espoused by Aristotle.

This short summary of some of the classical ethical theories is useful to understand which of the theories is more aligned to the concept of *ethics* presented in this book. It was found that virtue ethics is more related to the concept of *ethics* generated from the research that informed this book since it is the character of MLROs that determines their behaviour in either aligning with banks or regulators. In this regard, Kohlberg (1976) model of moral development is more fitting to the concept of *ethics* generated in this research because the author relies heavily on the writing of Aristotle (R Eric Reidenbach & Robin 1990), a strong proponent of virtue ethics.

Kohlberg (1973) formulated six stages of moral development categorised into pre-convention level (punishment-and-obedience and instrumental-relativist orientation), conventional level (interpersonal concordance and "law and order" orientation) and post conventional level (social-contract legalistic orientation). This model suggests that an individual moral development influences his decision relating to right and wrong and this *"provides a theoretical basis for understanding how managers think about ethical dilemmas"* (Trevino 1986 p. 602). This link between personal ethics corresponding to the stages of moral development and organisational ethics is particularly important since it aligns with the understanding of how MLROs are dealing with the conflict they face in complying with anti-money laundering regulations. This link was underlined by Trevino (1986 p. 608) who stated that *"based on prior research, it is expected that managers' reasoning about work-related ethical dilemmas is primarily at the conventional level (stages 3 and 4)"*.

Moreover, it was identified that personal ethics have a strong impact in influencing MLROs to align with regulators or banks, and this is consistent with the findings in Quinn (1997) and Trevino (1986) who found out that personal ethics is one of the factors that influences moral behaviour in organisations. But as discovered in the research, personal ethics alone does not translate into moral action, a distinction emphasised by Blasi (1980), since other contextual issues combine to influence the decision of an MLRO to act on his personal ethics. These contextual issues of culture, ego, characteristics of the work among others (Trevino 1986) are similar to the concepts of culture and unfair pressure presented in this book.

This distinction between moral reasoning and moral action (Blasi 1980) is important because MLROs may clearly see that the position of their banks on certain AML issues are against their personal ethics, but because of their *interest* they may not act on their personal ethics. Some MLROs that have strong personal ethics and convictions may, however, act on their personal ethics ignoring the contextual issues.

Furthermore, the research is not concerned with the relationship between ethics and performance, just as it is not focused on the relationship between culture and performance. The focus is about how ethics influences the decision of an MLRO in relation to dealing with regulators and banks in complying with AML regulations.

Self-Interest

Interest is another concept that was generated. Although the concept is broad and vague (Feldman 1982), the sense that it is used in this book is much more narrow, mainly focusing on the role of reward and punishment in influencing the decisions of an MLRO. This view aligns with the economic analysis of rational choice that assumes *"that a person commits an offense if the expected utility to him exceeds the utility he could get by using his time and other resources at other activities"* (Becker 1968 p. 176) but more appropriately the concept of self-interested attitude defined as *"one that is instrumental to the individual's attainment of valued goal"* (Sears et al. 1980 p. 671). The valued goal is related mainly to an MLRO's material well-being, reputation and family well-being.

Accordingly, it is the subjective interest of an MLRO that is relevant rather than the objective interest of regulators. The difference between the two is well described by Klonoski & Easton (1967 p. 45) who notes that subjective interest is, *"the interest of a person is to be found in his own interpretation of what is necessary if he is to realize his broader goal"*, while objective interest, *"may be described as those instrumental needs which others attribute to a person or group according to a criteria quite independent of the subjective perceptions of that person or group"* (Klonoski & Easton 1967 p. 45).

In addition, there are a number of studies suggesting that reward and punishment influence decision making (Andreoni et al. 2003; Oliver 1980; Sigmund et al. 2001). The issue, however, is the level of their influence. Andreoni et al. (2003) for example, suggested that most of the literature only focused on either reward or punishment, but that the combination of the two is more effective in influencing behaviour. Sigmund et al. (2001 p. 10758) on the other hand suggests *"that reputation is essential for fostering social behavior among selfish agents, and that it is considerably more effective with punishment than with reward"*.

Similarly, punishment is a core issue in the research by Becker (1968) in which he stated that the level of punishment and the type of punishment have strong influence on criminal behaviour with some having more influence than others. Andreoni et al. (2003) also found out that although reward influences behaviour, punishment has more influence on behaviour, but they also found that reward and punishment only partially explain the sources that influence behaviour. This is consistent with what is presented in this book, which found that although *interest* (*reward* and *punishment*) influences the aligning of an MLRO, there is belief (culture, ethic and conviction) that also influences behaviour.

There are other research studies that deal with reward and punishment based on the concept of collective reward and punishment, where the fault of one will affect others or the effort of one will benefits others (Heckathorn 1988). In this book, however, the concept of *interest* deals with individual *reward* and *punishment* in which an MLRO mainly receives reward from the bank in the form of remuneration and punishment from the regulators in the form of enforcement actions.

Similarly, there are research outputs that focus on selective incentives for collective action (Oliver 1980) rather that selective incentive for individual action which would be more appropriate. Although the idea of selective incentive aligned with the recommendation of fair treatment of MLROs, it is was discovered that there is not enough positive incentive from regulators to influence them to align with the regulators. Furthermore, incentives alone (reward and/or punishment) are not sufficient to influence their decision because of other factors, especially the concepts of *culture* and *ethics* discussed earlier.

Generation of a Theory

The theory of *self-protecting* is the main contribution of the book to literature. The significance of the theory is in its explanatory and predictive value. It is explanatory in that it explains the *discharging* behaviour of an MLRO, and it is predictive in that it suggests other behaviours based on the degree of *unfair pressure* on the MLRO.

Theories Earlier Discussed

As discussed in the preceding paragraphs, *self-protecting* has "integrative placement" with the various literature in the substance area of compliance. The self-protecting theory extends the theory of responsive regulation (Ayres & Braithwaite 1992) and voluntary compliance (Scholz 1984) by suggesting an optimal balance for compliance and enforcement. It suggested a modification to the legalistic quadrant of the tit-for-tat model to situate it in the compliance quadrant, suggested another form of tripartism with MLROs as the third parties instead of external third parties suggested by (Ayres & Braithwaite 1992) and generated a theoretical framework that explains compliance behaviour. Other integrated theories related with the *self-protecting* theory are the stakeholder mapping (Mendelow 1991) and agency theory (Jensen & Meckling 1976) in management, game theory in economics (Axelrod 1980) and socio-economic theory of regulation (Sutinen & Kuperan 1999).

Theories in Anti-Money Laundering

The theory of crying wolf (Takats 2011) and money laundering: the economics of regulation (Masciandaro 1999) in anti-money laundering are some of the relevant theories related with the theory of self-protecting.

The finding in Takats (2011 p. 32) that *"excessive fines force banks to report transactions which are less suspicious"* is similar to the concept of *unfair pressure*, but *self-protecting* is a broader theory that includes other compliance behaviour of MLROs and invariable the compliance behaviours of banks. The finding, however, is in line with the *discharging* behaviour of MLRO found in the book. One of Takat's recommendations to reduce fines may be one way of reducing unfairness which is part of the recommendation of this book, and the other recommendation for introducing reporting fees is also in line with the suggestion in *self-protecting* theory that fair pressure does not necessarily mean lack of pressure.

In Masciandaro (1999 p. 226), the main finding suggests that as *"legislation becomes more effective the less it is responsible for impairing the efficiency of banks"*. The main difference from the middle course approach is that Masciandaro (1999) is looking at efficiency in relation to banks and effectiveness in relation to regulators while the middle course approach is looking at effectiveness and efficiency in relation to both parties. The implicit assumption in the Masciandaro's research is that there is one common objective, which is to prevent money laundering. It was, however, shown that this assumption is not necessarily correct, as such it may not be appropriate to measure efficiency and effectiveness of one party based on the objective of another.

Theories in Psychology

The main contribution of the self-protecting in this regard is to link theories in psychology to AML. Firstly, the theory is related to the cognitive theory in psychology which emphasise the place of morality in compliance behaviour (Sutinen & Kuperan 1999). This is consistent with the concept of *belief* in which the *upstanding* of an MLRO sometime determines his alignment much more than the threat of *reward* or *punishment*. This is also in line with Kohlberg (1973) in which he argued that higher moral judgement stage is preferable to a lower level of moral development stage. The stages, from low to high, are: the punishment-and-obedience, the instrumental-relativist, the interpersonal concordance, the law and order, the social-contract legalistic and the universal-ethical-principle orientations.

Secondly, the self-preservation theory is also relevant to the *self-protecting* theory especially since the in vivo code of self-preservation was what gave rise to *self-protecting*. In general, self-preservation *"postulates that individuals make decisions so as to maximize the probability of their survival, and that they rank decision strategies according to this criterion alone"* (Karni & Schmeidler 1986 p. 72). The theory is, however, more of an evolutional theory that deals with the concern for survival and threat to life (de Catanzaro 1991) while the self-protecting theory is specific to regulatory behaviour. Self-preservation theory is, however, at a higher level of abstraction than the self-protecting theory given the wide application of the theory. Having said that, the concepts of self-protecting theory, such as unfair pressure, protecting, aligning, shifting expectation and marginal management are unique to the theory and, therefore, distinguished it from the self-preservation theory.

Thirdly, the protection motivation theory (PMT) is another theory that is related with the self-protecting theory. PMT is, however, concerned with resolving the *"fear appeal"* (Rogers 1975 p. 93) in which change in attitude is based on *"(a) the magnitude of noxiousness of a depicted event; (b) the probability of that eventâs occurrence; and (c) the efficacy of the protective response"*. The contribution of the *self-protecting* theory is that it conceptualised a tripartite relationship where there is a conflicting interest between two parties that have an effect on a third party whereas the protective motivation theory is a *"general theory of persuasive communication"* (Boer & Seydel 1996 p. 95) which serves as a communication tool for influencing behaviour. A *self-protecting theory* is, therefore, the theory of action and interaction between entities and not a way of persuasive communication to influence a decision. It is also a theory about resolving *unfair pressure* rather that fear. Similarly, the concepts of self-protecting theory are unique and this therefore distinguished it from the protection motivation theory.

Furthermore, the theory behind the fraud triangle in criminology is also similar to the self-protecting theory. The theory states that:

> Trusted persons become trust violators when they conceive of themselves as having a financial problem which is non-shareable, are aware that this problem can be secretly resolved by violation of the position of financial trust, and are able to apply to their own conduct in that situation verbalizations which enable them to adjust their conceptions of themselves as trusted persons with their conception of themselves as users of the entrusted funds or property. (Cressey 1953)

The summary of the theory is what is referred to as fraud triangle in which pressure, rationalisation and opportunity form the edges of the triangle (Turner et al. 2002). The theory is similar to the self-protecting theory because pressure corresponds to unfair pressure and rationalisation corresponds to justifying, a property of communicating. The difference, however, is that while the fraud triangle explains criminal behaviour, self-protecting theory deals with the behaviour of an MLRO who is an agent of the regulators to prevent criminal behaviour. In addition, pressure in fraud triangle is not categorised into fair and unfair pressure. In fraud theory, for example, it does not matter the type of pressure that give rise to a financial problem. If an individual has a non-shareable financial problem and has the opportunity because of his position of authority, he is likely to commit fraud and later rationalise his action. Introducing the distinction between fair and unfair pressure may extend the fraud theory by allowing law enforcement to understand the motivation behind a crime. A mother that steals money to treat her son who is dying of cancer should be viewed differently from a person who steals because of greed. By understanding the motivation behind the crime, law enforcement would be able to apportion blame not only on the mother that steals, but to the society that allows a mother to steal in order to take care of her son. Judges may also be lenient in their judgement because of the nature of pressure exerted on criminals that make them to commit crimes. Prosecutors may also decline to charge some suspects because of the nature of pressure on the suspects.

Theories in Organisation and Management

The study by R. Eric Reidenbach and Robin (1991) on organisational moral development shares important similarities with the *self-protecting* theory. Other theories in organisation and management include the agency and stakeholder theories.

Organisational Moral Development

R. Eric Reidenbach and Robin (1991) conceptualised five stages of moral development, that is, amoral, legalistic, responsive, ethical engaged and ethical organisational that are similar to the concepts situated in the self-protecting framework. Since *culture* and *ethics* are two of the concepts discovered in this research, it is important to bring the model to support the role of the two concepts in compliance behaviour.

Amoral organisation and legalistic organisation can be situated within the *discharging* quadrant with amoral being at the extreme end of *discharging*. Legalistic culture, however, aligns well with *discharging* since *"legalistic corporation so named because of the preoccupation the corporation exhibits for compliance with the letter of the law as opposed to the spirit of the law"*. (R. Eric Reidenbach & Robin 1991 p. 276). Responsive culture, on the other hand, is akin to *communicating* quadrant since *"responsive organizations begin to strike a balance between profits and doing right. However, doing right is still more of expediency rather than an end unto itself"*. This behaviour exerts *unfair pressure* on MLROs that make them *dialogue* constantly, *justify* their position and sometimes *threaten* their management in order to convince the organisation to comply with AML regulations.

In the same way, ethically engaged organisation corresponds to banks in the *complying* quadrant. This is so because their *culture "involves a recognition of a social contract between the business and society"* (R. Eric Reidenbach & Robin 1991 p. 279). The final stage called ethical organisations can also be situated in the *cooperating* quadrant. In these organisations, *"decisions are made based on the inherent justness and fairness of the decision as well as the profitability of the decision"*. (R. Eric Reidenbach & Robin 1991 p. 281). An MLRO in this organisation will be performing his duties since there is *fair pressure* from both the bank and the regulators.

The contribution of the *self-protecting* theory in this regard is, therefore, to link *culture* and *ethics* part of the theory to this model; first to show that the theory works and second to provide the understanding of how *ethics* and *culture* influence regulatory compliance. Although it is accepted that ethics influences compliance behaviour as summarised in R. Eric Reidenbach and Robin (1991), the *self-protecting* theory provides a framework that explains how it influences behaviour.

Other Related Theories

Agency Theory

Like the self-protecting theory, agency theory is also concerned with the problem of conflict of interest between parties (Wright & Mukherji 1999). Thus, agency theory is concerned with the principal agent relationship, and it assumes that the decision of individuals in the relationship is influenced by self-interest, bounded rationality and risk aversion (Eisenhardt 1989).

However, unlike the self-protecting theory that conceptualises the issue as a tripartite relationship by introducing a third party to mediate between the two parties with conflicting interests, agency theory is concerned with a bilateral relationship between the two contending parties. Furthermore, the solution to dealing with agency problem according to Eisenhardt (1989) is to align the interests of the two parties by structuring a contract between them in such a way that will deal with the agency problem of moral hazard and adverse selection on the one hand and risk sharing on the other. Self-protection theory, however, while recognising the value aligning conflicting interests, recognises that it may not be possible to align the interests, and as such introduces an independent third party to mediate the relationship between the two conflicting parties.

Although the self-protecting theory introduces MLROs as third parties in the relationship between regulators and banks, there is however an agency relationship between the regulators and the MLROs on the one hand and between the banks and the MLROs on the other hand. The agency relationship with the MLROs is, however, unlike the agency relation between the banks and the regulators because the interest of the MLROs and the banks is more aligned than between the bank and the regulator. Similarly, the interest of MLROs and the regulators is more aligned than the interest between the regulators and the banks. This was one of the findings of the research in which an independent MLRO that is treated fairly by both contending parties sits in the middle with the interest of both parties at heart.

Furthermore, the self-protecting theory not only explains the conflict of interest problem, but also suggests a theoretical solution to the problem called the middle course approach.

Stakeholder Theory

Stakeholder theory is an important theory that explains the relationship between a firm and others that it interacts with. According to Mitchell et al. (1997), the concept of stakeholder was introduced to the management literature with the publication of Strategic Management: A Stakeholder Approach by Freeman in 1984. The approach introduced other parties, both internal and external, that affect and are affected by a firm.

There are various explanations of the relationship between a firm and its stakeholders. Mitchell et al. (1997), for example, classifies stakeholders based on three attributes: power, legitimacy and urgency, while Savage et al. (1991) assesses stakeholders based on their potential to threaten or to cooperate with an organisation. It is, however, the Mendelow's power and interest matrix that is more related to the theory of self-protecting presented in this book. According to Mendelow (1991), stakeholders can be classified based on their level of interest and power. A stakeholder that has high power and high interest has high influence on a firm, while a stakeholder that has low power and low interest has a low influence on a firm. He proposed that high power, high interest stakeholders are key players while the strategy to adopt in dealing with low power and low interest stakeholders is to exert minimal effort. A stakeholder that is powerful but with low interest should however be kept satisfied while the one with high interest but low power should be kept informed.

The self-protecting theory is related to the stakeholder mapping in that they all recognised the effect of pressure on organisations. A stakeholder with high power and high interest can exert greater pressure on an organisation than a stakeholder with low power and low interest. What is however different between the two is that while pressure in stakeholder mapping is general, the pressure in self-protecting is categorised into fair and unfair. The outcome of a fair pressure is different from the outcome of an unfair pressure unlike in stakeholder mapping where this distinction is not made, and organisations adopt their strategies to deal with whatever pressure is exacted on them by the key player. This difference is even more important to the key player because exerting unfair pressure on a firm may lead the organisation to behave not in his interest, but to protect themselves by following the letter and not the spirit of the contract between them. If however he understands the difference between fair and unfair pressure and its impact on his own interest, he would know that it is only a fair pressure that can guarantee an outcome that is beneficial to him.

Drawing of Specific Implications

The specific implication of the self-protecting theory can be seen in diverse fields. In organisations, for example, it may have implication in any corporate organisation where there is conflicting pressure on an individual. Although the Mendelow's power and interest matrix (Mendelow 1991) is still relevant in dealing with different stakeholders, the self-protecting theory suggests a strategy that would protect the interest of the regulators as well as satisfying the organisation. This can be achieved by ensuring that pressure is fair on both the MLROs and the banks, which will then make banks and MLROs to cooperate in achieving the objective of the regulators.

The self-protecting theory may also have implications in health where doctors and nurses are dealing with conflicting pressure from patients and management who in turn are facing pressure from government and the public. This was highlighted by a nurse who lamented the conflicting pressure between doing what they believe is right and following rules. This is equally relevant to doctors who may have to suspend their discretion in order to follow rules and regulations.

Contribution to Rich Insight

One insight from the research that gave birth to this book is that it may not be a good idea to focus on aligning the interest of regulators and banks because it may be difficult to do so since they have conflicting interests. Although aligning the interest of regulators and banks may be the best option in theory, it may not be a good idea in practice.

One of the contributions of the book is to suggest the middle-course approach that allows the two conflicting objectives to coexist. By acknowledging that banks and regulators have different objectives, an effective compliance policy can be established that treats MLROs with fairness and gives them the required independence to perform their roles.

Another insight is the concept of isomorphism, which relates the desire for an ideal situation where the interest of regulators and banks is aligned towards preventing money laundering.

Pressure is also the subject of the theory of institutional isomorphism. Although the theory identified three mechanisms, that is coercive, mimetic and normative isomorphism (DiMaggio & Powell 1983), it is the coercive isomorphism mechanism that is more relevant to this research. The concept is defined as follows: *'coercive isomorphism results from both formal and informal pressures exerted on organizations by other organizations upon which they are dependent'* (DiMaggio & Powell 1983 p. 150). Their focus is, however, *'what makes organisations similar?'* While this research is focused on how some individuals (MLROs) within organisations react to pressure and the impact it has on compliance. The concept of fairness attached to pressure will, therefore, extend the concept of coercive isomorphism to alert those with coercive powers the opportunity to mould other organisations to behave in the way that is beneficial to all parties. In AML for, example, a fairer system of regulation would make AML more effective and efficient as suggested by the middle course approach discussed in this chapter.

By implementing a fair coercive isomorphism, for example, regulators would ensure that regulated firms cooperate fully in the fight against money laundering. Coercive isomorphism is the use of pressure on a dependant organisation to conform to the objectives of an independent organisation. Instead of coercing banks by using tough regulation, regulators can exert fair pressure to ensure that firms are willingly complying with AML regulations.

Finally, the use of simple solutions for the complex problems may be better and more efficient than the current use of expensive technology that is ineffective (Demetis 2010).

Conclusion

Several concepts that formed the self-protecting theory were presented in this book. These concepts contribute in understanding compliance behaviours. Unfair pressures, for example, would affect how an individual behaves, while the concept of marginal management explains the difficulty in dealing with employees not under a person's direct control. Shifting expectation is also another concept that explains the frustration of compliance officers in dealing with regulators. Understanding these concepts and adopting measures to deal with them will go a long way to ensure an effective and efficient regulatory regime.

Besides these concepts, which are unique, there are other concepts generated that share some similarities with existing concepts in the literature. Some of the existing concepts are organisational culture, belief, ethics and self-interest. The integration of these concepts into the self-protecting theory further explains the concepts in a different light, therefore, extending their application.

The main contribution of this book is, however, in generating a theory that is both explanatory and predictive. It explains the behaviour of compliance officers to AML regulations and also predicts that kind of behaviour that they will exhibit in certain situations. This will help policy makers to structure regulations and policies that would make MLROs more supporting in the fight against money laundering. The theory is also related to other theories in the literature such as the Crying Wolf theory in AML, Self-preservation theory and Protection Motivation theory in psychology and Organisational Moral Development in organisation and management.

Another contribution of the book is in the application of the self-protecting theory in other industries such as health where doctors and nurses are in similar situations to that of compliance officers. There is also a contribution to rich insight, especially as regards the idea that it is always better to align the interest of parties with conflicting interest. Even though this book does not doubt the efficacy of this approach, there are instances where it may not be possible to do so, in which case it is better to recognise that fact and develop solutions that would accommodate the conflicting interests.

In summary, this chapter presented the contribution of the self-protecting theory by integrating the theory into relevant literature. The self-protecting theory was compared with similar theories in AML, psychology, organisation and management to show its contribution. The general implication of the theory and its contribution to rich insight were also highlighted so also the significance of some key concepts generated from the research.

7

Conclusion

Introduction

In Chap. 1 of this book, the purpose of the book, the summary of the self-protecting theory and the potential significance of the book were discussed. Chapter 2 provided the context relating to AML, the UK regulatory environment and the role of MLROs to enable a proper appreciation of the emergent theory. In Chap. 3, the self-protecting theory, which states that the more unfair pressure on MLROs the more they protect themselves rather than prevent money laundering, was presented. The self-protecting framework discovered from the study was also presented in the chapter, which showed the predictive feature of the theory. In Chaps. 4 and 5, the theory was integrated into the general literature related to it using the middle-course approach, a recommended approach for effective compliance. Chapter 6 highlighted the additional contribution of the self-protecting theory by showing its general application in other areas and the rich insights it provides.

A.U. Bello, *Improving Anti-Money Laundering Compliance*,
Palgrave Studies in Risk, Crime and Society,
DOI 10.1007/978-3-319-43264-9_7

This chapter presents the conclusion of the book. It starts by summarising the emergent theory of self-protecting and the key concepts that make up the theory. The theoretical contribution of the book is highlighted as well as the significance of the book. The chapter also presents how the aims and objectives of the book were achieved before finally discussing the limitation of the book and implication for future research.

Summary of the Emergent Theory

The research underpinning this book has applied a grounded theory approach to the following two questions:

1. What is the main concern of MLROs?
2. How are they resolving their main concern?

In order to achieve this, the author followed the procedures of classical grounded theory by concurrently collecting and analysing data, writing and sorting memos and integrating the concepts discovered to generate the self-protecting theory.

The self-protecting theory is, therefore, a theory on how MLROs are dealing with their main concern as compliance officers in the UK banking industry. During the course of the research, the concept of *unfair pressure* emerged as the main concern of MLROs.

Unfair Pressure – Main Concern

Unfair pressure emerged as the main concern out of the desire of MLROs to balance two competing interests, one from the side of banks and one from regulators. Accordingly, unfair pressure was subdivided into regulatory concerns and organisational concern to separate the two sources of concerns.

Regulatory concerns, on the one hand, include defective regulation, shifting expectation, damage to reputation and naive regulators. The risk based approach and the consent and sanction regimes were particularly identified as part of the regulation that is defective. The other complaint relates to constant changes in regulation and the expectation of regulators. There are also some implicit expectations of regulators based on their own interpretation of laws, but not necessarily based on the fact of the law. This implicit and explicit regulatory expectation was conceptualised as shifting expectation. Another concern is the potential damage to their reputation. MLROs complained about the constant threat of prosecution, personal liability and bad image associated with the job. Finally, on regulatory concerns, they complained about the naivety of regulators. They argued that some regulators do not have the experience, skill and understanding to regulate the industry due in part to lack of resources and high staff turnover.

Organisational concerns, on the other hand, mainly relate to under resources and marginal management. They complained about the lack of time because, in addition to being MLROs, most have multiple roles while for those who are only responsible for MLRO function, they may be responsible for AML in other countries that have a different regulatory environment. The most important concerns related to under resource concern, however, relate to lack of adequate investment in systems and controls to deal with changing technology and innovative money laundering schemes. In addition, they complained about lack of required support from other employees and inadequate compensation.

The other major concern is *marginal management*. This is a new concept that highlights the concerns of MLROs as regards the difficulty in managing colleagues that are not directly under their control. An MLRO necessarily has to deal with other department such as marketing department, information technology and front office. The concern, however, is that MLROs do not have the necessary authority to deal with these members of staff who have other priorities and who, in some instance, are at par with them in terms of hierarchy.

Protecting – A Way of Resolving the Concern over Unfair Pressure

Depending on the type of pressure and its source, MLROs will be aligning with banks or regulators. If the unfair pressure is from regulators, for example, then MLROs will mainly be aligning with banks and vice versa. *Aligning* as a category has two properties, *interest* and *belief*. The interest of MLROs determines their alignment, and it has *reward* and *punishment* as its two properties. *Reward* is mainly in terms of salary from banks and recognition from regulators while *punishment* is mainly in terms of the threat of prosecution and damage to reputation from the actions of regulators and loss of job and uncertainty of getting a job after redundancy from actions of banks. *Belief*, on the other hand, relates to the conviction of the MLRO on what is right and wrong, the culture in the organisation that influences the MLRO and the ethical orientation of the MLRO. While most MLROs are upstanding because of their background reflected in their career choice and their compliance behaviour, few are not as upright.

Protecting

MLROs adopt various strategies to deal with their concerns. The core category that is used to deal with *unfair pressure* is the *protecting* behaviour, which is designed to protect an MLRO from the organisational and regulatory pressure they face. The main ways of *protecting* are through *discharging* when dealing with regulators and *communicating* when dealing with banks.

Discharging

MLROs' main strategy for discharging is by assessing a transaction to see whether it is suspicious or not. MLROs, when assessing, are trying to find a balance between the interest of regulators to prevent money laundering and the interest of banks to increase profitability. The decision to assess an activity as suspicious is easy for obvious cases of suspicious transactions. In other situations, however, where the decision is not that straightforward, MLROs use their *discretion* to decide whether an activity is suspicious or not. The use of *discretion* is based mainly on available information, guidance and resources, but most importantly, it is based on the *interest* and *belief* of the MLROs. If their *interest* is best served by *aligning* with regulators then they are more likely to assess an activity as suspicious, but if their *interest* is best served by aligning with banks then they are less likely to assess it as suspicious.

After *assessing* an activity, an MLRO then decides to report or not to report the activity. The two properties of *reporting* are *playing safe* in which the MLRO chooses an easier decision that best serves his interest and *defending* for the difficult choices that he has to defend either in term of reporting an activity that the bank does not feel he should report or not reporting an activity that the regulators feel he should report. These two properties are mainly used to deal with concerns over defective regulation, shifting expectation and damage to reputation.

Assessing and *reporting* are, therefore, the two main properties of *discharging*. *Automating, learning* and *complaining* are the other properties of *discharging*. *Automating* is a means for *assessing* and *reporting* by using software and technology to support the *assessing* and *reporting* activities. *Learning* is also similar to *automating* in that MLROs are regularly engaged in formal and informal activities to acquire the necessary skills and knowledge to enable them perform their duties. Some of the activities include attending training and attending conferences and seminars. In all these activities, MLROs are always looking for opportunities to network with each other in order to gain insight and share experiences. The final property of *discharging* for dealing with regulatory concern is *complaining*. *Complaining*, in addition to being a method for identifying concerns, is used by MLROs as a means for expressing their concern to relieve themselves of what is on their mind. They are happy to find a sympathetic ear that would listen to their concerns.

Communicating

When dealing with banks, the *communicating* strategies for MLROs are *dialogue, justifying, threat* and *complaining*. The first strategy is *dialogue*, which involves *negotiating* with management for resources and *negotiating* with colleagues for support and shared resources. The second way for dealing with unfair organisational pressure is by *justifying* their action to management as regards reporting suspicious activities, demand for extra resources and the decision to disallow a profitable business because of a concern over money laundering. MLROs, as a last resort, threaten management for lack of adequate resource and threaten employees with the threat of prosecution if they fail to support their activities. They also find solace in *complaining* about under resources and lack of support from other employees.

Even though there are instances of *communicating* behaviour by some MLROs in the UK, MLROs are mostly *discharging* their responsibility to protect themselves from the regulators rather that *complying* with regulation to prevent money laundering. Even though this is the situation in the UK, the *self-protecting* theory has predictive value, which suggests that in an environment that has more unfair organisational pressure; MLROs will be *communicating* to protect themselves rather than *cooperating* with banks to protect the interest of the banks. Based on this descriptive and predictive value of the theory, a framework was discovered that has four quadrants namely *discharging* behaviour, *communicating* behaviour, *complying* behaviour and *cooperating* behaviour.

Self-Protecting Framework

A *discharging* behaviour implies an environment where MLROs are more aligned with banks and most of the unfair pressure is coming from regulators; a *communicating* behaviour implies a situation where MLROs are more aligned with regulators and most of the unfair pressure is coming from banks. The situation where there is more fair pressure from regulators and MLROs more aligned with regulators indicates *complying* behaviour and finally a situation where most of the fair pressure is from banks and MLROs are aligning with banks signifies *cooperating* behaviour.

Since the study is about compliance activities and MLROs, whose role is specified in regulation, the theory translates into a regulatory strategy, in addition to a compliance strategy. In this regard, the *discharging* behaviour corresponds to *weak* regulation because of the unfair pressure from regulators that make MLROs care more about protecting themselves than *preventing* money laundering. Similarly, the *communicating* quadrant corresponds to *tough* regulation because of the unfair pressure from banks, and the *complying* quadrant corresponds to *smart* regulation because the fair pressure from the regulators. Finally, the *cooperating* quadrant corresponds to self-regulation because of fair pressure from banks.

The framework is, however, a predictive model, which does not identify the best approach for effective and efficient compliance. To recommend a better enforcement strategy, the middle-course approach was discovered which is a position on the framework in-between *smart regulation* that is effective for the regulators but not necessarily efficient and *self-regulation* that is effective for banks but not necessarily efficient. Accordingly, the middle-course approach is a regulatory strategy that recommends giving MLROs more independence and treating them with fairness. This is the recommendation of the research that emerges from the self-protecting theory.

Contribution to Knowledge

In grounded theory where a full theory is discovered, it is expected that contributions will be made (Urquhart 2013). This is because it will be difficult if not impossible to find in the literature a theory with the same concepts and the same relationship between concepts as the grounded theory (Glaser 1978). The theory will, however, be similar to other theories but, even so, there will be enough differences to ensure contribution to knowledge as seen in Chap. 5. In the following section, the summary of the potential contributions of self-protecting to knowledge and practice is discussed.

Theoretical Contribution

The research has generated a theory about a substantive area of AML that lacks theoretical foundation. In addition, the self-protecting theory has both explanatory and predictive value. It explains the current AML environment in the UK from the perspective of one of the major stakeholders (MLROs) and predicts a different situation that may occur in a different regulatory environment.

These explanatory and predictive values are conceptualised in the self-protecting framework, which is a model that can be used to identify the regulatory environment in a country based of the actions of stakeholders in that country. Furthermore, the study has recommended a middle-course approach as an alternative approach to the deterrence and the self-regulatory view of compliance.

The above contributions can be better explained as follows:

Generation of Concepts

Three concepts are selected for discussion to show the contribution of the self-protecting theory to knowledge. The concepts are *unfair pressure*, *shifting expectation* and *marginal management.*

Unfair Pressure

The first is *unfair pressure*, which is the main concern of MLROs about AML compliance in the UK. This concept is a combination of two independent concepts; *unfair* and *pressure* that were initially generated separately but after further analysis it was discovered that combining them together explains the main concern of MLROs. Thus, this combination is one of the main contributions of the theory. This is because unfair is already an established concept in the literature especially legitimacy literature in sociology (Sutinen & Kuperan 1999; Tyler 2006). The concept is aligned the concept of procedural justice in which individuals prefer the process of regulation to be fair much more that the outcome of the process (Sutinen & Kuperan 1999; Tyler 2006). Similarly, pressure is also an established concept. In management, for example, the nature of power and interest of a stakeholder determines the strategy a company should adopt (Mendelow 1991). Stakeholders that have high power and high interest will exert pressure on the company, and as such, the company should design strategies to manage them closely. Pressure is also a concept in isomorphism, a theory that explains what makes organisations similar. Coercive isomorphism, a type of isomorphism that suggests the use of coercive pressure by independent organisations on dependent organisations (DiMaggio & Powell 1983), is the closest to the concept of pressure identified in the book.

The contribution of unfair pressure, therefore, is to combine the two concepts together to give a different meaning from the established concepts in the literature. In the Mendelow matrix and isomorphism, for example, the emphasis is not whether pressure is fair or not, and in procedural justice, fair is a broad concept that included fairness that is not a result of pressure. In addition, fairness in legitimacy theory relates to the actual potential criminals while unfair pressure deals with MLROs who are agents rather than targets of regulation.

Marginal Management

Marginal management is a concept generated to capture the difficulty that MLROs face when dealing with employees in other departments that are not under their direct control. It is a major concern to MLROs because the nature of their job entails that they have to interact regularly with other departments and, in some cases, they may have to make decisions that would not be acceptable to others. This type of relationship has not been the subject of research as downward and upward management has been. The closest concept to marginal management is the flat structure that encourages cooperation and teamwork. The difference with marginal management, however, is that often the objective of MLROs is at variance with that of other departments such as marketing, for example, that is more concerned with opening customer accounts. Other departments' objectives are also more aligned to the objectives of the organisation, but for an MLRO department, their objective of reporting suspicious activities may conflict with the main objective of the bank of making profit.

Another contribution of the marginal management is that it may provide a concept for other employees in similar situations to MLROs. For example, internal auditors and other compliance officers may be facing a similar problem, which can be explained by the concept of marginal management.

Shifting Expectation

The final concept is *shifting expectation*. It encompasses the problem of information overload and changing regulatory expectation that may be familiar to many compliance officers. Shifting expectation is a problem in which regulators constantly change regulations, introduce new guidelines and produce huge documents, which they expect MLROs to go through and implement. The problem is exacerbated because, despite the huge volume of materials and the high expectation of the regulators, MLROs are often not allowed to use their discretion when making judgments. *Shifting expectation* may also apply to organisations that deal with multiple stakeholders such as not-for profit organisation that have to satisfy the need of their donors or sponsors, the demand of their customers and the regulatory requirements. The contribution of the concept is, therefore, to conceptualise the concerns of a wide range of people, especially compliance officers, that is then resolved using the *protecting* strategy.

Generation of a Theory

The self-protecting theory is related to several theories in various disciplines. It relates to game theory in economics, legitimacy theory in sociology and regulation in anti-money laundering. It also relates to cognitive theory, self-preservation theory and protecting motivation theory in psychology and stakeholder theory, agency theory and ethics in organisation and management.

Regulatory Theories

The most evident contribution of the theory is in regulation. This is because the self-protecting theory was discovered within the substantive area of AML regulation. The relevant theories related to the self-protecting theory include responsive regulation, voluntary compliance, deterrence theory, legitimacy theory and AML regulation.

Responsive regulation (Ayres & Braithwaite 1992) introduces the concept of NGO as independent third parties to assist in enforcing compliance. This book, however, proposes giving MLROs as much independent as necessary to be able to ensure compliance. The advantage of this approach over employing external third parties is that MLROs are already part of the system and, as such, they have the experience, skills and commitment for the job. Being part of the system and having the skills and training for the job would also save resources and time that would be require if external NGOs are to be involved in a process that they may not have the capacity to handle.

The self-protecting theory also suggested a modification to the application of games theory to regulation. In Scholz (1984), for example, it was recognised that the best strategy for effective compliance was voluntary compliance, which is similar to self-regulation strategy of the self-protect framework. Other strategies include temptation, which corresponds to weak regulation in which firms are benefiting at the expense of regulators; harassment in which regulators and benefiting at the expenses of firms and confrontation in which both are not getting the optimal benefit that voluntary compliance would offer. The study, however, suggests an alternative approach that combines the best of self-regulation and smart regulation to produce a middle-course approach that may increase the effectiveness of enforcement and the efficiency of compliance.

A link to the deterrence theory of Becker (1968) was also highlighted in which the concept of *interest* which has *reward* and *punishment* as its properties aligns with the deterrence theory. Self-protecting theory, however, added the concept of *belief*, which has *culture*, *ethics* and *conviction* at its properties, to suggest a modification to the deterrence theory. Self-protecting theory accepts the deterrence approach, but it also accepts the legitimacy approach to regulation. The theory of legitimacy that closely aligns with the self-protecting theory is the procedural justice, which *"involves how fairly the authority treats people and the concerns of those affected by the process" (Sutinen & Kuperan* 1999 *p. 183).* The contribution of the self-protecting theory in this regard is combining deterrence model and procedural justice approach to form a socio-economic theory of regulation.

Money Laundering

There are two theories in AML that aligned closely with the self-protecting theory namely the theory of crying wolf and the economic theory of money laundering. The first relates to the concepts of *discharging* which is similar to the concept of crying wolf in which excessive reporting was identified as a problem in AML (Takats 2011). The author argues that excessive fine "force *banks to report transactions which are less suspicious*" (Takats 2011 p. 32). The contribution of the self-protecting theory is to conceptualise the problem to include not only excessive fines, but also other concerns that can be covered by the concept of unfair pressure. In addition, the self-protecting theory provides a framework in which further research can be undertaken to identify other indications of unfairness to inform change in policies.

The economic theory of money laundering regulation, on the other hand, links effectiveness of enforcement with efficiency of compliance (Masciandaro 1999). The self-protecting theory adds to this by suggestion a similar focus on efficiency of enforcement and effectiveness of compliance. This contribution was demonstrated by the middle-course approach in which it was suggested that the objective of banks and regulators are different as such the view of effectiveness and efficiency by one is not necessarily the same view by the other. The author, like others in the literature, is more concerned with effectiveness of enforcement and efficiency of compliance while the self-protecting theory widens the context to look at effectiveness and efficiency form both perspectives. In addition, self-protecting theory views the problem of AML, not from banks-regulators perspective but rather, from the perspective of MLROs who are often regarding as part of banks but who are discovered sometimes to have different interest from the interest of banks.

Theories in Psychology

Theories in psychology also greatly relate to the self-protecting theory. The self-preservation theory is one example of this relationship. The contribution of the self-protecting theory is, however, to relate the self-preservation theory to regulation and focus on a different concern of unfair pressure from the concern of survival in self-preservation (de Catanzaro 1991). The self-preservation is, however, a higher-level theory that encompasses the self-protecting theory as regard the protecting behaviour of MLRO.

Similarly, self-protecting theory is related to the protection motivation theory. Although they are similar in name, they differed in the nature of the problem they address and their application. The self-protecting theory is about dealing with unfair pressure to protect oneself, whereas the protecting motivation theory is a persuasive theory that deals with the concern of fear (Boer & Seydel 1996 p. 95).

Other theories in this field that relate and integrate with the self-protecting theory include the cognitive theory (Kohlberg 1973), which related the concept of *belief* generated in the research to a higher level of moral development.

Theories in Organisation

The stakeholder mapping and agency theory are the two major theories that are related to the self-protecting theory. The stakeholder mapping of Mendelow (1991) supports the concept of pressure, but it did not differentiate between a fair pressure and an unfair pressure. The Mendelow matrix assumes that when a stakeholder has high power and interest, an organisation is better advised to manage the stakeholder in its own interest. Self-protecting theory is, however, suggesting that it is only when the pressure, represented by power and interest, is fair that the stakeholder would gain the optimal value from the relationship otherwise the organisation will be discharging its responsibilities but not necessarily serving the interest of the stakeholder.

Similarly, the self-protecting theory suggests that MLROs should beseen more as agents of banks, on the one hand, and regulators, on the other, and should be treated as such. The prevalent view of the position of MLRO is that they are part of banks and, therefore, share the same interest. This view has some merit in that they are more aligned with the banks than with regulators as seen earlier in Chap. 3, but they also have other interests different from the interest of their banks that may make them to align with regulators rather than banks.

A final theory that is relevant to the self-protecting theory is the organisation moral development theory (R. Eric Reidenbach & Robin 1991). The five stages of moral development, that is, Amoral, legalistic, responsive, ethically engaged and ethical organisations, support the concept of *belief* that has *ethics*, culture and *conviction* as its property. The moral development theory shows that the concept of belief works, but it only explains a part of the self-protecting theory.

Self-Protecting: An Introduction to a Formal Theory

Self-protecting theory is a substantive theory of MLROs. It can however be upgraded to become a formal theory that deals with self-protecting in general. A formal theory can best be explained by an example. According to Glaser (2008 p. 16), for example, "*becoming a nurse, a substantive theory, can be generalized to becoming a professional, a formal theory, and even raised to a higher formal level of becoming in general, a theory of socialization*".

It is not the intention of the author to present a formal theory in this book because the aim of the book is to present a substantive theory and its implication. It is, however, important to highlight the relationship between a self-protecting as a substantive grounded theory and self-protecting as a potential formal theory, which will show the contribution of self-protecting theory in the discovery of a formal theory.

In the following section, the potential for a formal theory will therefore be explored.

Implication in Organisations

Dealing with this conflict can happen in other corporate organisations when management has to deal with conflicts in stakeholder's interest. This might happen in organisations where management is pursuing a strategy for growth and profitability to satisfy shareholders, but also adopting strategies to deal with regulators and pressure groups that have conflicting objectives. The nature of pressure would probably determine the strategy to adopt much more than the power and the interest of the stakeholders. A powerful stakeholder with high interest in an organisation can exert maximum pressure to protect its interest, but if the interest is considered unfair, management may adopt a *discharging* behaviour than to align with the interest of the stakeholder.

Implication in the Health Industry

Self-protecting theory is also applicable in the health sector where doctors and nurses are dealing with conflicting interest from patients that are demanding proper care, on the one hand, and management that wants to save cost. This insight was first identified when the author was presenting the self-protecting theory at a seminar in the US. A nurse in the audience stated that what the author said is what is happening in the hospital where she works. She gave an example of dealing with patient in a triage situation. She wants to follow instructions concerning prioritising treatment, but she also wants to supports other patients who are less in need of support but who are equally suffering from their pains. Consistent with research in virtue ethics in nursing (Smith & Godfrey 2002), she believes it is unfair to place nurses in a situation where they have to choose between following instructions and helping patients (Personal Communication 2013).

Similarly, doctors might be in a similar situation as described in (TEDxStanford 2012) where a patient suffering from cancer was given several treatment options to choose from instead of the doctor using his discretion to treat the patient. One possible explanation for doctors' behaviour is that they *"want to protect themselves legally"* since it is a legal requirement, for some aliments, to inform patients about treatment options (Guadagnoli & Ward 1998). This protecting behaviour is in line with the concept of *discharging* of the *self-protecting* theory.

Contribution to Rich Insight

The theory of self-protecting also provides insight in other areas that are not the focus of this book. It seems, for example, that *aligning* the interest of banks and regulators to a common objective may not be the solution to preventing money laundering after all, since it may not be feasible to reconcile the differences. Another option is to have fair pressure on a compliance officer who would then ensure that both parties benefit from a more effective regulation.

The concept of isomorphism mentioned is also another area that deserves attention. If some MLROs are complaining that regulations are developed for political reasons, then the theory may shed more light on the role of international organisations like the FATF in promoting policies that may be seen to be promoting the interest of some members of the organisation at the expense of others.

The use of simple solutions to deal with money-laundering problems is another insight gained from the book. According to one of the participants, for example, there is an organisation that provides AML service where an MLRO will speak with an experienced person who will ask a series of questions regarding a potential suspicious transaction and then provide useful advice on how to deal with the situation based on his experience and information available to him. The participants stated that the £750 paid for subscribing to the service was the best value for money investment he has made as an MLRO. This was also the argument at TEDSalon (2010) that simple solutions are sometimes more potent than much more expensive solutions. The following anecdotal example was given, " *those strange little signs that actually flash '35'at you, occasionally accompanying a little smiley face or a frown, according to whether you're within or outside the speed limit – those are actually more effective at preventing road accidents than speed cameras, which come with the actual threat of real punishment*".

Similarly, another participant advocates the use of a "*common sense*" approach to AML regulation especially relating to the use of software. He stated "*I always use this analogy. There is no point of having an expensive system if you don't have the skilled personnel to handle it. It is like giving my small daughter a Royce Royce to drive*". According to him, common sense is better than using expensive software for preventing money laundering. This is also the argument by Demetis (2009 p. 358) who characterised the use of automation in AML as "*reckless utilisation of AML software*".

The table below (Table 7.1) summarises some of the contributions of the research behind the book:

Table 7.1 Contribution of the research

Area of contribution	Authors	Supported	Added	Challenged	New
Economics	(Becker 1968)	The concept of utility is similar to the concept of interest discover n this study	Unlike Becker's theory, however, this research recognised the role of belief in shaping compliance behaviour	The notion that social factors do not matter is challenged since belief is a key concept discovered in the research	
		Becker's deterrence model can also be situated within the communicating quadrant of the self-protecting framework which indicates tough regulation			

(*continued*)

Table 7.1 (continued)

Area of contribution	Authors	Supported	Added	Challenged	New
Sociology	(Tyler 2006)	The author confirms the importance of belief in compliance behaviour. His emphasis on procedural justice as a way of evaluating legitimacy aligns with the concept of unfair pressure discovered in this research The theory of Tyler corresponds to the cooperating quadrant of the self-protecting framework which emphasise the important of cooperation between the regulators and the regulated		This research is not completely convinced that social issues are the main driver of compliance behaviours since it was shown that reward and punishment play a very important part in deciding the aligning of an MLRO	This research focuses on MLROs who are not the ultimate target of AML provision while Tyler's study is focused on individuals that are the direct target of regulation

Area of contribution	Authors	Supported	Added	Challenged	New
Socio-economic	(Scholz 1984)	The voluntary compliance strategy of Scholz corresponds with the cooperation quadrant of the self-protecting theory which suggests a self-regulation approach	The complying quadrant of self-protecting frameworkadded a new dimension to the confrontation strategy of Scholz. While confrontation is seen as bad for the regulators and the regulators, complying suggest that it is a better approach than discharging and communicating		The research introduces a fifth approach that is suggested to be an alternative approach to the voluntary compliance approach proposed by Scholz

(continued)

Table 7.1 (continued)

Area of contribution	Authors	Supported	Added	Challenged	New
		The temptation and harassment strategies in Scholz model also corresponds to discharging and communicating quadrants in the self-protecting framework	While the view in Scholz study is on the effectiveness of enforcement and efficiency of compliance, this study views the issue from the effectiveness and efficiency of enforcement and effectiveness and efficiency of compliance		This research focuses on MLROs who are not the ultimate target of AML provision while Scholz's study is focused on individuals that are direct target of regulation
	(Ayres & Braithwaite, 1992)	The enforced self-regulation of Ayers & Braithwaite is similar to the cooperating quadrant of the self-protecting framework which implies self-regulation	Instead of the external independent third parties suggested by Ayers & Braithwaite, this study recommends making MLROs the third parties		This study is focused on individuals while responsive regulation of Ayres is focused on organisation.

Area of contribution	Authors	Supported	Added	Challenged	New
			While the view in Ayers & Braithwaite study is on the effectiveness of enforcement and the efficiency of compliance, this study views the issue from the effectiveness and efficiency of enforcement and the effectiveness and efficiency of compliance		The research introduces a fifth approach called middle-course approach that is suggested to be an alternative approach for AML compliance

(*continued*)

Table 7.1 (continued)

Area of contribution	Authors	Supported	Added	Challenged	New
Money laundering	(Takats 2011)	The finding in Takats that suggest that excessive fine is making banks report less suspicious activities is similar to the concept of discharging generated in the research.	Self-protecting is, however, broader since discharging is one out of many concepts. The concept of communicating, for example, where the unfair pressure is coming from the bank, is not explained by the Takats' theory		The focus of the Takats' theory is also on the banks rather than on individuals, in this case MLROs. The new insight from this research is that MLROs are to some extent distinct from banks.
		One of the recommendations of the author to reduce fine is also similar to the concept of reducing unfair pressure			

Area of contribution	Authors	Supported	Added	Challenged	New
	(Masciandaro 1999)		The self-protecting theory added the concept of effectiveness and efficiency for the perspective of both banks and regulators rather than assuming there is one objective, which is to prevent money laundering		The research recommends the middle-course approach as an alternative compliance approach

(*continued*)

Table 7.1 (continued)

Area of contribution	Authors	Supported	Added	Challenged	New
Psychology					
	(Karni & Schmeidler 1986), (de Catanzaro 1991)	The self-preservation is similar to the self-protecting theory as regard protecting the interest of an individual. The concerns are, however, different. While the concern in self-protecting theory is unfair pressure the concern in self-preservation is survival	The self-protecting theory also links the general idea of protecting self to the AML environment		

Area of contribution	Authors	Supported	Added	Challenged	New
	(Rogers 1975)	The self-protecting theory also supports the protection motivation theory. The concern is, however, different while self-protecting theory deals with unfair pressure the protection motivation theory deals with fear appeal	The application of the protection motivation theory is mainly in the area of persuasion while the self-protecting theory is a theory that explains compliance behaviour.		
			Even though the PMT has wide application, fear a concern in PMT is only one of the concerns of an MLRO related to damage to reputation		

(continued)

Table 7.1 (continued)

Area of contribution	Authors	Supported	Added	Challenged	New
Organisation and management	(Reidenbach & Robin 1991)	Robin's theory of organisation moral development is similar to the self-protecting framework in which the five stages are mapped to the framework that is Amoral and legalistic like discharging; responsive with communicating; ethically engaged with complying; ethical organisation to cooperating.	The self-protecting, therefore, added a new dimension by linking organisation moral development to compliance behaviour of MLROs represented by the concept of belief		

Source: Author

Significance of the Book

This book looked at the problem of AML compliance from the point of view of MLROs. This is significant because most books in this area looked at the relationship between banks and regulators by assuming that MLROs are part of banks. The responses from participants, however, showed that this is not entirely an accurate assessment. Although they are more aligned with the banks than the regulators, they sometimes have conflicting interest with their banks, especially when the banks have a weak culture. It is, therefore, important to view MLROs as distinct as possible from their banks when formulating AML policies.

Perhaps the most significant insight of the research is the discovery of a theory on how the conflicting interest between banks and regulators affect an MLRO. This conflicting interest, sometimes, results in unfair pressure on MLROs, which then make them to devise strategies for protecting themselves rather than serving the interest of either banks or regulators. Furthermore, this conflicting pressure may be applied in similar situations where an individual is dealing with competing interest between various stakeholders. Regulators may, therefore, adopt better policies by recognising areas of conflicting unfair pressure.

The significance of discovering a theory in AML is underlined by the call by Nardo (2006) for a theoretical foundation in the field of money laundering and other financial crimes. He argues that an "*appropriate theory can lead to prompter and more effective action, or prevent the waste time and resources in trying to achieve empirically something we can never attain*" (Nardo 2006 p. 292).

Achieving the Aims of the Book

The rigorous process adopted for the research underpinning this book starting from identifying the paradigm of research and the resulting methodology, followed by adhering to the tenets of the classical grounded methodology in discovering the self-protecting theory ensured that the aims and objectives of the book were achieved.

The following is the summary of the aims and objectives of the book:

1. Understand the AML environment from the perspective of MLRO.
2. Discover concepts from their perspective that will explain their concerns and the ways of resolving them.
3. Identify the main concern and the core category that resolves it.
4. Build a theory that would explain how MLROs resolve their main concerns.
5. Discover a framework that will explain the environment in which they operate.
6. From the framework, suggest an effective and efficient approach to AML compliance,

The first objective was achieved through interacting with participants, listening to their concerns and conceptualising their behaviours to discover a theory and a framework that explains how they are dealing with their concerns. Through the grounded theory process, concepts were generated that identified the concerns and the strategies MLROs are adopting to deal with them. Some of the concepts generated are presented in (Table 7.2) below:

Out of these concepts, *unfair pressure* was identified as the main concern of MLROs, which encompasses the other concepts under it.

Table 7.2 Key concepts

Unfair pressure	Protecting	Aligning
• Defective regulation	• Discharging	• Belief
• Shifting expectation	• Assessing	• Culture
• Damage to reputation	• Reporting	• Conviction
• Naïve regulator	• Learning	• Ethics
• Under resources	• Automating	• Interest
• Marginal management	• Complaining	• Reward
	• Communicating	• Punishment
	• Dialog	
	• Justifying	
	• Threat	
	• Complaining	

Source: Author

Likewise *protecting* was discovered as the core category for resolving the unfair pressure concern. These two concepts answered the third objective, which was to identify the main concern of participants and the core category for resolving it. In addition, *aligning* is a sub-core concept of *protecting* that indicates whether MLROs are *protecting* themselves against banks or regulators.

The theoretical codes of degree and paired opposite were then used to integrate the main concern and the core category into a self-protecting theory that suggests that the more unfair pressure is exerted on MLROs, the more they protect themselves. This theory answers the fourth objective of discovering a theory that explains how MLROs are resolving their main concern. Furthermore, a framework was discovered to answer the fifth objective of discovering a framework that explains the environment in which they operate. It was found that the AML regulatory environment in the UK is generally *weak* with MLROs *discharging* their responsibility to protect themselves rather than *complying* with regulation to prevent money laundering. A middle-course approach was proposed to achieve the last objective of recommending an effective approach for improving the AML compliance in the UK. The middle-course approach suggests that the more independence is given to MLROs and the more they are treated fairly, the more AML compliance will be more effective.

Finally, the self-protecting theory and the framework are based on the perspectives of MLROs. A formal theory can, however, be discovered by looking at the concerns of other stakeholders to discover a more comprehensive theory that would explain the whole AML environment in the UK. The recommendations from the research underpinning the book can also be implemented by regulators. Regulators, for example, may introduce regulations that are considered fair from the perspective of MLROs or repeal laws that are considered unfair. The consent regime, for example, is an area that may need to be amended to remove the threat of prosecution to MLROs. MLROs can also be given some level of independence to enable them perform their roles effectively. One of the suggesting from the data is for regulators to share in the payment of salaries of MLROs thereby ensuring that MLROs are not sympathetic to one party the expense of the other.

Evaluating the Self-Protecting Theory

Although there are various criteria for evaluating social research (Elliott & Lazenbatt 2005; Hammersley 2013; Mays & Pope 2000; Murphy et al., 1998), Glaser (1978 p. 4), however, insisted that the only criteria that should be used to assess the quality of a grounded theory is that it *"must have fit and relevance, and it must work.... A theory must also be modifiable"*. He emphasised that a theory *"does not have to be legitimized beyond these humble boundaries"*. In another place, he stated "*there is no need to preamble grounded theory to distraction with the promise of legitimacy. Let the product legitimize itself*" (Glaser 1998 p. 16). Because of this, the self-protecting theory may be viewed in relation to these criteria.

The four criteria for evaluating a grounded are, therefore, fitness, relevance, workability and modifiability. Firstly, fitness refers to the ability of categories generated to fit the data. In Chap. 3, several examples were given on how concepts were discovered from the data through a rigorous process of constant comparison. Secondly, a theory works if it is *"able to explain what happened, predict what will happen and interpret what is happening in the area of substantive or formal enquiry."* (Glaser 1978 p. 4). In Chaps. 3 and 5, the self-protecting theory, the framework and the middle-course approach were presented to show the workability of the theory in the substantive area of AML and regulation in general. Thirdly, *"grounded theory arrives at relevance, because it allows core problems and processes to emerge"* (Glaser 1978 p. 5). In Chap. 3, it was shown how the core category was identified, and how memos were sorted and integrated, using two theoretical codes, to form the self-protecting theory. The rigorous process that ensured the emergence of the theory, the framework and the middle-course approach is also a testimony of the relevance of the theory. Finally, generating a theory *"is an ever modifying process and nothing is sacred if the analyst is dedicated to giving priority to data"* (Glaser 1978 p. 5). Discovering the theory of self-protecting has undergone a series of modifications as more data is collected and analysed. Even when the theory was at the final stage of discovery, further analysis was conducted, memos were sorted and resorted and concepts were redefinedto fit the data. At the end, the theory can still be modified if, after the research, further data emerged that would require the theory to be modified.

The workability, relevance and modifiability of the theory can further be established in future research using the self-protecting framework. The theory can be tested by conducting a research on MLROs in other countries, MLROs in other sectors or other stakeholder in the AML industry.

It is hoped that the book has demonstrated the fitness, workability, relevance and modifiability of the self-protecting theory.

Limitation of the Book

As with all classical grounded theory studies, the aim of the study is not description but conceptualisation (Glaser 2002) as such the essence of participants' experience was not described in detail, as would be the case in a phenomenological study, for example (Creswell 2007). The author, however, followed rigorous procedures to achieve the aim of the book, which was to generate a theory that explains how MLROs are resolving their main concern.

Even though the author has followed a rigorous approach to generate the theory, a theory in grounded theory is always modifiable. More data can be gathered, and different stakeholders can be included in addition to MLROs. Restricting the research to one stakeholder, however, ensured that a grounded theory was discovered that fits, is workable and relevant within the sampled data.

Finally, the author conducted the research while learning the process. Even though the learning process came early in the research, the author does not have previous experience of conducting a grounded theory research. This limitation was, however, reduced by attending specialised training, reading core texts of the methodology and following the core procedures of the approach.

Implication for Further Research

It has already been mentioned that the self-protecting theory can be used as a theoretical framework to conduct research in various countries, different sectors and in different disciplines. This general implication of the research is indicated by the number of theories in different fields that relate to it as discussed in Chap. 6. The potential for further research is, therefore, immense.

The middle-course approach discovered can also be considered, at least in the UK, to find out if it works. Furthermore, research can be conducted based on the self-protecting theory using the self-protecting framework to confirm its workability and relevance. A formal theory can also be discovered based on similar theories in other disciplines to find a more comprehensive theory of regulation.

In addition, some key concepts such as marginal management, shifting expectation and unfair pressure can be further explored to find out their full potential in explaining regulatory behaviours in AML and other regulatory situations.

Conclusion

It may be evident from the above discussion that the book has been able to achieve its set aims and objectives. This was done by adhering to the procedures of classical grounded theory in collecting, analysing and discovering the self-protecting theory. As a result of this, the research was able to contribute to knowledge and practice by introducing a relevant theory that works and by recommending an approach for effective compliance.

References

Allan, G. (2003). A critique of using grounded theory as a research method. *Electronic Journal of Business Research Methods, 2*(1), 1–10.

Andreoni, J., Harbaugh, W., & Vesterlund, L. (2003). The carrot or the stick: Rewards, punishments, and cooperation. *American Economic Review*, 893–902.

Araujo, R. A. (2008). Assessing the efficiency of the anti-money laundering regulation: An incentive-based approach. *Journal of Money Laundering Control, 11*(1), 67–75.

Aristoteles. (1893). *The Nicomachean Ethics*. p. 359.

Arvai, J. L. (2007). Rethinking of risk communication: Lessons from the decision sciences. *Tree Genetics & Genomes, 3*(2), 173–185.

Axelrod, R. (1980). Effective choice in the prisoner's dilemma. *The Journal of Conflict Resolution, 24*(1), 3–25. doi:10.2307/73932

Ayres, I., & Braithwaite, J. (1991). Tripartism: Regulatory capture and empowerment. *Law & Social Inquiry, 16*(3), 435–496.

Ayres, I., & Braithwaite, J. (1992). *Responsive regulation: Transcending the deregulation debate*. Oxford: Oxford University Press.

Baldwin, R., & Cave, M. (1999). *Understanding regulation: Theory, strategy, and practice*. Oxford: Oxford University Press.

A.U. Bello, *Improving Anti-Money Laundering Compliance*,
Palgrave Studies in Risk, Crime and Society,
DOI 10.1007/978-3-319-43264-9

Barley, S. R., Meyer, G. W., & Gash, D. C. (1988). Cultures of culture: Academics, practitioners and the pragmatics of normative control. *Administrative Science Quarterly*, *33*, 24–60.

Barone, R., & Masciandaro, D. (2011). Organized crime, money laundering and legal economy: Theory and simulations. *European Journal of Law and Economics, 32*(1), 115–142.

Basel. (1988). *Prevention of criminal use of the banking system for the purpose of money-Laundering*. http://www.bis.org/list/bcbs/tid_32/index.htm

Basel. (2001). *Customer due diligence for banks*. Basel: Bank of International Settlements.

Basel. (2004). *Consolidated KYC risk management*. Bank of International Settlements.

Bauman, Z. (2003). *Intimations of postmodernity*. London: Taylor & Francis.

Becker, G. S. (1968). Crime and punishment: An economic approach. *Journal of Political Economy*, *76*(2), p. 169.

Bentham, J. (1825). *The rationale of reward*. London: John and H. L. Hunt.

Bentley, A. F. (1967). *The process of government* (1908). Cambridge, MA: Harvard University Press.

Bergstrom, M., Helgesson, K. S., & Morth, U. (2011). A new role for for profit actors? The case of anti money laundering and risk management. *JCMS: Journal of Common Market Studies, 49*(5), 1043–1064.

Blasi, A. (1980). Bridging moral cognition and moral action: A critical review of the literature. *Psychological Bulletin, 88*(1), 1–45. doi:http://dx.doi.org/10.1037/0033-2909.88.1.1

Boer, H., & Seydel, E. R. (1996). Protection motivation theory. In M. Conner & P. Norman, (Eds.), Predicting health behaviour: Research and practice with social cognition models. Buckingham: The Open University, pp. 95–120.

Bosworth-Davies, R. (1998). Living with the law: A survey of money-laundering reporting officers and their attitudes towards the money-laundering regulations. *Journal of Money Laundering Control, 1*(3), 245–253.

Canhoto, A. I. (2008). Barriers to segmentation implementation in money laundering detection. *The Marketing Review, 8*(2), 163–163.

Clarke, A. E., & Friese, C. (2007). Grounded theorizing using situational analysis. In A. Bryant & K. Charmaz (Eds.), *The SAGE handbook of grounded theory*. SAGE Publications.

Cleveland, C., Hogan, C., & Saundry, P. (2010). Deepwater horizon oil spill. *The encyclopedia of earth*. http://www.eoearth.org/view/article/161185

Cooke, R. A., & Rousseau, D. M. (1988). Behavioral norms and expectations. A quantitative approach t. *Group & Organization Studies, 13*(3), 245.
Corbin, J., & Strauss, A. (1990). Grounded theory research: Procedures, canons, and evaluative criteria. *Qualitative Sociology, 13*(1), 3–21.
CPS. (2010, 15/09/10). Proceeds Of Crime Act 2002. http://www.cps.gov.uk/legal/p_to_r/proceeds_of_crime_money_laundering/
Cressey, D. R. (1953). Other people's money; a study of the social psychology of embezzlement.
Creswell, J. W. (2007). *Qualitative inquiry & research design: Choosing among five approaches* (2nd ed. ed.). Thousand Oaks: Sage Publications.
Crow, D. R., & Liggett, D. P. (2014). Beliefs drive behaviors. *Industry Applications, IEEE Transactions on, 50*(2), 1530–1536. doi:10.1109/TIA.2013.2288213
de Catanzaro, D. (1991). Evolutionary limits to self-preservation. *Ethology and Sociobiology, 12*(1), 13–28. doi:http://dx.doi.org/10.1016/0162-3095(91)90010-N
de Koker, L. (2009). Identifying and managing low money laundering risk. *Journal of Financial Crime, 16*(4), 334–352.
de Wit, J. (2007). A risk-based approach to AML: A controversy between financial institutions and regulators: A controversy between financial institutions and regulators. *Journal of Financial Regulation and Compliance, 15* (2), 156–165.
Deal, T. E., & Kennedy, A. A. (1988). *Corporate cultures: The rites and rituals of corporate life*. Harmondsworth: Penguin.
Demetis, D. S. (2009) Data growth, the new order of information manipulation and consequences for the AML/ATF domains. *Journal of Money Laundering Control, 12*(4), 353–353.
Demetis, D. S. (2010). *Technology and anti-money laundering: A systems theory and risk-based approach*. Northampton, USA: Edward Elgar Publishing.
Demetis, D. S., & Angell, I. O. (2007). The risk-based approach to AML: Representation, paradox, and the 3rd directive. *Journal of Money Laundering Control, 10*(4), 412–428.
Denison, D. R. (1990). *Corporate culture and organizational effectiveness*. New York: John Wiley & Sons.
Denison, D. R., & Mishra, A. K. (1995). Toward a theory of organizational culture and effectiveness. *Organization Science, 6*(2), 204–223.
Denzin, N. K., & Lincoln, Y. S. (2005). *The SAGE Handbook of Qualitative Research*. London: SAGE Publications.

DiMaggio, P., & Powell, W. W. (1983). The iron cage revisited: Institutional isomorphism and collective rationality in organizational fields. *American Sociological Review, 48*(2), 147–160.

Dion, M. (2012). Are ethical theories relevant for ethical leadership? *Leadership & Organization Development Journal, 33*(1), 4–24. doi:10.1108/01437731211193098

Dolar, B., & Shughart II, W. F. (2011). Enforcement of the USA Patriot Act's anti-money laundering provisions: Have regulators followed a risk-based approach? *Global Finance Journal, 22*(1), 19–31.

Edwards, J., & Wolfe, S. (2005). Compliance: A review. *Journal of Financial Regulation and Compliance, 13*(1), 48–59.

Egmont Group. (2000). *FIUs in action: 100 cases from the Egmont Group*. Canada. Egmount Group.

Egmont Group. (2012). *2011–2012 Annual Report*. Canada. Egmont Group

Eisenhardt, K. M. (1989). Agency theory: An assessment and review. *Academy of Management Review, 14*(1), 57–74.

Elliott, N., & Lazenbatt, A. (2005). How to recognise a 'quality' grounded theory research study. *The Australian Journal of Advanced Nursing: A Quarterly Publication of the Royal Australian Nursing Federation, 22*(3), 48.

European Union. (1991). *Council Directive 91/308/EEC of 10 June 1991 on prevention of the use of the financial system for the purpose of money laundering*. http://eur-lex.europa.eu/LexUriServ/LexUriServ.do?uri=OJ:L:1991:166:0077:0082:EN:PDF.

European Union. (2001). *Directive 2001/97/EC of The European Parliament and of the Council of 4 December 2001 amending Council Directive 91/308/EEC on prevention of the use of the financial system for the purpose of money laundering*. http://eur-lex.europa.eu/LexUriServ/LexUriServ.do?uri=OJ:L:2001:344:0076:0081:EN:PDF.

European Union. (2005). *Directive 2005/60/EC of the European Parliament and of the Council of 26 October 2005 on the prevention of the use of the financial system for the purpose of money laundering and terrorist financing*. http://eur-lex.europa.eu/LexUriServ/LexUriServ.do?uri=OJ:L:2005:309:0015:0036:EN:PDF.

European Union. (2013). *Money Laundering in Europe*. Luxembourg. European Union.

European Union. (2015). Directive (EU) 2015/849 of the European Parliament and of the Council. http://eur-lex.europa.eu/legal-content/EN/TXT/?uri=CELEX%3A32015L0849

FATF. (1990). *The Forty Recommendations*. Paris. Financial Action Task Force.

FATF. (2005). *FATF Annual Report 2004–2005*. Paris. Financial Action Task Force.

FATF. (2007a). *FATF Annual Report 2006–2007*. Paris. Financial Action Task Force.

FATF. (2007b). *Guidance on the risk-based approach to combating money laundering and terrorist financing: High level principles and procedures*. Paris: Financial Action Task Force.

FATF. (2007c). *Third mutual evaluation report—Anti-money laundering and combating the financing of terrorism, The United Kingdom of Great Britain and Northern Ireland*. Paris. Financial Action Task Force.

FATF. (2012). *FATF Recommendations*. Paris. Financial Action Task Force.

FATF. (2013a). *FATF Annual Report 2012–2013*. Paris. Financial Action Task Force.

FATF. (2013b). FATF Public Statement—21 June 2013. http://www.fatf-gafi.org/topics/high-riskandnon-cooperativejurisdictions/documents/public-statement-june-2013.html

FATF. (2013c). *What do we do*. http://www.fatf-gafi.org/pages/aboutus/whatwedo/

Favarel-Garrigues, G., Godefroy, T., & Lascoumes, P. (2008). Sentinels in the banking industry: Private actors and the fight against money laundering in France. *British Journal of Criminology, 48*(1), 1–19.

Favarel-Garrigues, G., Godefroy, T., & Lascoumes, P. (2011). Reluctant partners? Banks in the fight against money laundering and terrorism financing in France. *Security Dialogue, 42*(2), 179–196.

Feldman, S. (1982). Economic self-interest and political behavior. *American Journal of Political Science, 26*(3), 446–466. doi:10.2307/2110937

Financial Conduct Authority. (2013a). *Anti-money laundering annual report 2012/2013*. https://www.fca.org.uk/publication/corporate/anti-money-laundering-report.pdf

Financial Conduct Authority. (2013b). *Handbook: SYSC*. http://fshandbook.info/FS/html/FCA/.

Financial Services Authority. (2012). *Final Notice: Habib b Bank AG Zurich*. Financial Services Authority.

Financial Service Authority. (2012a). *Decision Notice: Turkish Bank (UK) Ltd*. http://www.fsa.gov.uk/static/pubs/final/turkish-bank.pdf.

Financial Service Authority. (2012b). *Final Notice: Habib Bank AG Zurich*. http://www.fsa.gov.uk/static/pubs/final/habib-bank.pdf

Financial Services Authority. (2011). *Financial conduct authority: Approach to regulation.* http://www.fsa.gov.uk/pubs/events/fca_approach.pdf
Fishbein, M., & Ajzen, I. (1975). *Belief, attitude, intention and behavior: An introduction to theory and research.* London (etc.): Addison-Wesley.
Friedman, L. M. (1985). On Regulation and Legal Process. In R. G. Noll (Ed.), *Regulatory policy and the social sciences (pp. 111–135).* California: University of California Press.
Garvin, D. A. (1984). What does 'product quality' really mean. *Sloan Management Review, 26*(1), 25–43
Geiger, H., & Wuensch, O. (2007). The fight against money laundering: An economic analysis of a cost-benefit paradoxon. *Journal of Money Laundering Control, 10*(1), 91–105.
Gibbs, C., Gore, M. L., McGarrell, E. F., & Rivers, L., III. (2010). Introducing conservation criminology: Towards interdisciplinary scholarship on environmental crimes and risks.(Author abstract). *British Journal of Criminology, 50*(1), 124.
Glaser, B. (1978). *Theoretical sensitivity: Advances in the methodology of grounded theory.* Mill Valley, CA: Sociology Press.
Glaser, B. (1998). *Doing grounded theory: Issues and discussions.* Mill Valley, CA: Sociology Press.
Glaser, B. (1999). The future of grounded theory. *Qualitative Health Research, 9*(6), 836–845.
Glaser, B. (2001). *The grounded theory perspective: Conceptualization contrasted with description.* Mill Valley, CA: Sociology Press.
Glaser, B. (2002). Constructivist grounded theory? *3*(3). http://www.qualitative-research.net/index.php/fqs/article/view/825
Glaser, B. (2005). *The grounded theory perspective III: Theoretical coding.* Mill Valley, CA: Sociology Press.
Glaser, B. (2008). Conceptualization: On theory and theorizing using grounded theory. *International Journal of Qualitative Methods, 1*(2), 23–38.
Glaser, B. (2011). *Getting out of the data: Grounded theory conceptualization.* Mill Valley, CA: Sociology Press.
Glaser, B. (2012). *Stop. write! writing grounded theory.* Mill Valley, CA: Sociology Press.
Glaser, B., & Holton, J. (2005). Staying open: The use of theoretical codes in grounded theory. *The Grounded Theory Review, 5*(10), 1–20.
Glaser, B., & Strauss, A. (1965). Discovery of substantive theory: A basic strategy underlying qualitative research. *American Behavioral Scientist, 8*(6), 5–12.

Glaser, B., & Strauss, A. (1967). *The discovery of grounded theory: Strategies for qualitative research*. New York: Aldine de Gruyter.

Goldby, M.A. (2012). Anti-money laundering reporting requirements imposed by English law: Measuring effectiveness and gauging the need for reform. *Journal of Business Law*, Forthcoming.

Grabosky, P. N. (1995). Counterproductive regulation. *International Journal of the Sociology of Law, 23*(4), 347–369. doi:http://dx.doi.org/10.1016/S0194-6595(05)80003-6

Guadagnoli, E., & Ward, P. (1998). Patient participation in decision-making. *Social Science & Medicine, 47*(3), 329–339. doi:http://dx.doi.org/10.1016/S0277-9536(98)00059-8

Guerron-Quintana, P. A. (2012). Risk and uncertainty. *Business Review (Federal Reserve Bank of Philadelphia)*, 10, Q1, 2012.

Gurd, B. (2008). Remaining consistent with method? An analysis of grounded theory research in accounting. *Qualitative Research in Accounting & Management, 5*(2), 122–138. doi 10.1108/11766090810888926

The Money Laundering Regulation 2007, No. 2157 C.F.R. (2007).

Haimes, Y. Y. (2009). On the complex definition of risk: A systems-based approach. *Risk Analysis, 29*(12), 1647–1654. doi:10.1111/j.1539-6924.2009.01310.x

Hammersley, M. (2013). *What's wrong with ethnography?* New York: Taylor & Francis.

Harvard Law Review. (1993). The bureaucrats of rules and standards. *106*, 1685–1690. Harv. L. Rev. http://heinonline.org

Harvey, J. (2008). Just how effective is money laundering legislation? *Security Journal, 21*(3), 189–211.

Harvey, J. (2009). The search for crime money-debunking the myth: Facts versus imagery. *Journal of Money Laundering Control, 12*(2), 97–100.

Harvey, J. & Bosworth-Davies, R. (2016). Drawing the line in the sand: Trust, integrity and regulatory misdemeanor. *Security Journal*, 29, 367. doi:10.1057/sj.2013.33; First Online: 2013.

Harvey, J., & Lau, S. F. (2009). Crime-money, reputation and reporting. *Crime, Law and Social Change, 52*(1), 57–72.

Heckathorn, D. D. (1988). Collective sanctions and the creation of prisoner's dilemma norms. *American Journal of Sociology, 94*, 535–562.

Hinterseer, K. (2001). The Wolfsberg anti-money laundering principles. *Journal of Money Laundering Control, 5*(1), 25.

Hursthouse, R. (1999). *On virtue ethics*. New York: Oxford University Press.

Hyde, A. (1983). Concept of legitimation in the sociology of law. *The. Wis. L. Rev.*, 379.

Jackson, A. (2000). Recognising and reporting money laundering: How well should you know your customer? *Journal of Money Laundering Control, 3*(4), 317–324.

Jackson, P. (2012). *Value for money and international development: Deconstructing myths to promote a more constructive discussion*. Paris: OECD.

Jensen, M. C., & Meckling, W. H. (1976). Theory of the firm: Managerial behavior, agency costs and ownership structure. *Journal of Financial Economics, 3*(4), 305–360.

JMLSG. (2011). *Guidance for the UK financial sector: Part I*. http://www.jmlsg.org.uk/industry-guidance/article/guidance

JMLSG. (2014). *What is JMLSG?* http://www.jmlsg.org.uk/what-is-jmlsg

Jones, R., & Noble, G. (2007). Grounded theory and management research: A lack of integrity? *Qualitative Research in Organizations and Management: An International Journal, 2*(2), 84–103.

Kant, I. (1964). *Groundwork of the metaphysic of morals*. trans. HJ Paton. New York: Harper & Row, pp. 420–426.

Karni, E., & Schmeidler, D. (1986). Self-preservation as a foundation of rational behavior under risk. *Journal of Economic Behavior & Organization, 7*(1), 71–81. doi:http://dx.doi.org/10.1016/0167-2681(86)90022-3

Kelle, U. (2005). 'Emergence' vs. 'forcing' of empirical data? A crucial problem of 'grounded theory' reconsidered. *2005, 6*(2). http://www.qualitative-research.net/index.php/fqs/article/view/467

Killick, M., & Parody, D. (2007). Implementing AML/CFT measures that address the risks and not tick boxes. *Journal of Financial Regulation and Compliance, 15*(2), 210–216.

Klonoski, J. R., & Easton, D. (1967). A systems analysis of political life. *The Western Political Quarterly*, (Vol. 20). doi:http://doi.org/10.2307/446211.

Kohlberg, L. (1973). The claim to moral adequacy of a highest stage of moral judgment. *The Journal of Philosophy, 70*(18), 630–646. doi:10.2307/2025030

Kohlberg, L. (1976). Moral stages and moralization: The cognitive development developmental approach. In C. Beck & E. Sullivan (Eds.), *Moral Education*. Toronto: University of Toronto Press.

Kono, T., & S. R. Clegg. (1998). *Transformations of corporate culture: Experiences of Japanese enterprises*. Berlin: Walter de Gruyter.

Kotter, J. P. (2008). *Corporate culture and performance*. Simon and Schuster.

KPMG. (2011). *Global anti-money laundering survey 2011: How banks are facing up to the challenge*. Switzerland.

Kraut, R. (1994). *Desire and the human good.* Paper presented at the Proceedings and Addresses of the American Philosophical Association.
Kroszner, R. S., & Strahan, P. E. (1999). What drives deregulation? Economics and politics of the relaxation of bank branching restrictions. *The Quarterly Journal of Economics, 114*(4), 1437–1467.
Kunda, G. (2009). *Engineering culture: Control and commitment in a high-tech corporation.* Philadelphia: Temple University Press.
Laffont, J.-J., & Tirole, J. (1991). The politics of government decision-making: A theory of regulatory capture. *The Quarterly Journal of Economics, 106*(4), 1089–1127. doi:10.2307/2937958
Levi, M., & Reuter, P. (2006). Money laundering. *Crime and Justice—A Review of Research, 34*(34), 289–375. <Go to ISI>://000260691400006
Markus, H. R., & Kitayama, S. (1991). Culture and the self: Implications for cognition, emotion, and motivation. *Psychological Review, 98*(2), 224–253. doi:http://dx.doi.org/10.1037/0033-295X.98.2.224
Marshall, P. (2004). Part 7 of the Proceeds of Crime Act 2002: Double criminality, legal certainty, proportionality and trouble ahead. *Journal of Financial Crime, 11*(2), 111–126.
Masciandaro, D. (1999). Money laundering: The economics of regulation. *European Journal of Law and Economics, 7*(3), 225–240.
Masciandaro, D., & Barone, R. (2008). Worldwide anti-money laundering regulation: Estimating the costs and benefits. *Global Business & Economics Review, 10*(3), 243–264. doi:10.1504/GBER.2008.019983
Masters, J. L. (2008). Fraud and money laundering: The evolving criminalization of corporate non-compliance. *Journal of Money Laundering Control, 11* (2), 103–122.
Mays, N., & Pope, C. (2000). Qualitative research in health care: Assessing quality in qualitative research. *BMJ: British Medical Journal, 320*(7226), 50. http://www.ncbi.nlm.nih.gov/pmc/articles/PMC1117321/pdf/50.pdf
McCann, T. V., & Clark, E. (2003). Grounded theory in nursing research: Part 1—Methodology. *Nurse Rsearcher, 11*(2), 7.
Mendeloff, J. (1993). Overcoming barriers to better regulation. *Law & Social Inquiry, 18*(4), 711–729.
Mendelow, A. (1991). *'Stakeholder Mapping'.* Paper presented at the Proceedings of the 2nd International Conference on Information Systems, Cambridge, MA.
Mill, J. S. (1870). Utilitarianism. London: Longmans, Green.

Mitchell, R. K., Agle, B. R., & Wood, D. J. (1997). Toward a theory of stakeholder identification and salience: Defining the principle of who and what really counts. *Academy of Management Review, 22*(4), 853–886.

Mitsilegas, V., & Gilmore, B. (2007). The EU legislative framework against money laundering and terrorist finance: A critical analysis in the light of evolving global standards. *International and Comparative Law Quarterly, 56*(1), 119.

Murphy, E., Dingwall, R., Greatbatch, D., Parker, S., & Watson, P. (1998). Qualitative research methods in health technology assessment: A review of the literature. *Health Technology Assessment (Winchester, England), 2*(16), 3.

Nardo, M. (2006). Building synergies between theory and practice. *Journal of Financial Crime, 13*(3), 292–299.

National Crime Agency. (2013a). About us. http://www.nationalcrimeagency.gov.uk/about-us

National Crime Agency. (2013b). *Obtaining consent from the NCA under Part 7 of the Proceeds of Crime Act (POCA) 2002 or under Part 3 of the Terrorism Act (TACT) 2000.* http://www.nationalcrimeagency.gov.uk/publications/24-obtaining-consent-from-the-nca/file

National Crime Agency. (2013c). *Submitting A Suspicious Activity Report (SAR) within the Regulated Sector.* http://www.nationalcrimeagency.gov.uk/publications/61-submitting-a-sar/file

National Crime Agency. (2014). SARs legal basis for reporting. http://www.nationalcrimeagency.gov.uk/about-us/what-we-do/specialist-capabilities/ukfiu/legal-basis-for-reporting

New York District Attorney. (2012). *Standard chartered bank reaches $327 million settlement for illegal transactions.* New York. http://manhattanda.org/press-release/standard-chartered-bank-reaches-327-million-settlement-illegal-transactions.

Nussbaum, M. C. (1988). Non-relative virtues: An Aristotelian approach. *Midwest Studies in Philosophy, 13*(1), 32–53.

Oliver, P. (1980). Rewards and punishments as selective incentives for collective action: Theoretical investigations. *American Journal of Sociology*, 85, 1356–1375.

Orb, A., Eisenhauer, L., & Wynaden, D. (2001). Ethics in qualitative research. *Journal of Nursing Scholarship, 33*(1), 93–96. doi:10.1111/j.1547-5069.2001.00093.x

Ouchi, W. G., & Price, R. L. (1978). Hierarchies, clans, and theory Z: A new perspective on organization development. *Organizational Dynamics, 7*(2), 25–44. doi:http://dx.doi.org/10.1016/0090-2616(78)90036-0

Peters, T. J., author., & Waterman, R. H., author. (2006). *In search of excellence: Lessons from America's best-run companies* (Collins Business Essentials edition. ed.). New York: HarperCollins.

Proceeds of Crime Act (2002).

Prosser, T. (2006). Regulation and social solidarity. *Journal of Law and Society, 33*(3), 364–387. doi:10.1111/j.1467-6478.2006.00363.x

Punch, M. (1994). Politics and ethics in qualitative research. *Handbook of Qualitative Research, 2*, 83–98.

Quinn, J. (1997). Personal ethics and business ethics: The ethical attitudes of owner/managers of small business. *Journal of Business Ethics, 16*(2), 119–127. doi:10.1023/A:1017901032728

R. v. Rollins [2010] UKSC 39.

Reeve, C. D. C. (2014). *Nicomachean ethics*. Indiana: Hackett Publishing Company, Incorporated.

Reidenbach, R. E., & Robin, D. P. (1990). Toward the development of a multidimensional scale for improving evaluations of business ethics. *Journal of Business Ethics, 9*(8), 639–653.

Reidenbach, R. E., & Robin, D. P. (1991). A conceptual model of corporate moral development. *Journal of Business Ethics, 10*(4), 273.

Reuter, P., & Truman, E. M. (2004). *Chasing dirty money: The fight against money laundering*. Washington, DC: Peterson Institute.

Rhodes, R., & Palastrand, S. (2004). A guide to money laundering legislation. *Journal of Money Laundering Control, 8*(1), 9.

Rogers, R. W. (1975). A protection motivation theory of fear appeals and attitude change1. *The Journal of Psychology, 91*(1), 93–114.

Ross, S., & Hannan, M. (2007). Money laundering regulation and risk-based decision-making. *Journal of Money Laundering Control, 10*(1), 106–115.

Ryder, N. (2008). The financial services authority and money laundering a game of cat and mouse. *The Cambridge Law Journal, 67*(3), 635–653. doi:10.1017/S0008197308000706

Ryder, N. (2012). *Money laundering: An endless cycle*. Abingdon: Routledge.

Saffold, G. S. (1988). Culture traits, strength, and organizational performance: moving beyond 'strong' culture. *Academy of Management Review, 13*(4), 546–558. doi:10.5465/AMR.1988.4307418

Sathye, M., & Islam, J. (2011). Adopting a risk-based approach to AMLCTF compliance: The Australian case. *Journal of Financial Crime, 18*(2), 169–182.

Savage, G. T., Nix, T. W., Whitehead, C. J., & Blair, J. D. (1991). Strategies for assessing and managing organizational stakeholders. *The Executive, 5*(2), 61–75.

Sayre-McCord, G. (2012). Coherentism and the justification of moral beliefs. *Ethical Theory: An Anthology, 14*, 112.

Schein, E. H. (2004). The role of the founder in creating organizational culture. *Modern Classics on Leadership, 443*.

Schein, E. H. (2010). *Organizational culture and leadership*. San Francisco, CA: Wiley.

Schneider, F., & Windischbauer, U. (2008). Money laundering: Some facts. *European Journal of Law and Economics, 26*(3), 387–404. doi:10.1007/s10657-008-9070-x

Scholz, J. T. (1984). Voluntary compliance and regulatory enforcement. *Law & Policy, 6*(4), 385–404. doi:10.1111/j.1467-9930.1984.tb00334.x

Scholz, J. T. (1993). Review: responsive regulation: transcending the deregulation debate. *The American Political Science Review, 87*(3), 782–783. doi:10.-2307/2938772

Schott, P. A. (2006). *Reference guide to anti-money laundering and combating the financing of terrorism*. Washington, DC.

Schroeder, W. R. (2001). *'Money laundering' a global threat and the international community's response*. Washington DC: FBI Law Enforcement Bulletin.

Sears, D. O., Lau, R. R., Tyler, T. R., & Allen Jr, H. M. (1980). Self-interest vs. symbolic politics in policy attitudes and presidential voting. *The American Political Science Review, 74*(3), 670–684.

Selznick, P. (1985). Focusing organizational research on regulation. In R. G. Noll (Ed.), *Regulatory policy and the social sciences. California:* University of California Press.

Shafer-Landau, R. (2007). *Ethical Theory: An Anthology*. Wiley.Shah v HSBC Private Bank (UK) Limited [2012] EWHC 1283.

Sharman, J. C. (2008). Power and discourse in policy diffusion: Anti-money laundering in developing states. *International Studies Quarterly, 52*(3), 635–656. doi:10.1111/j.1468-2478.2008.00518.x

Shehu, A. Y. (2005). International initiatives against corruption and money laundering: An overview. *Journal of Financial Crime, 12*(3), 221–245.

Sigmund, K., Hauert, C., & Nowak, M. A. (2001). Reward and punishment. *Proceedings of the National Academy of Sciences, 98*(19), 10757–10762. http://www.ncbi.nlm.nih.gov/pmc/articles/PMC58548/pdf/pq010757.pdf

Singer, P. (1974). All animals are equal. *Philosophic Exchange*, 5(1), 6.

Slote, M. (1995). Agent-based virtue ethics. *Midwest Studies in Philosophy, 20*(1), 83–101.

Smith, K. V., & Godfrey, N. S. (2002). Being a good nurse and doing the right thing: A qualitative study. *Nursing Ethics, 9*(3), 301–312.

Solomon, R. C. (1992). Corporate oles, personal virtues: an Aristotle approach to business ethics. *Business Ethics Quarterly, 2*(3), 317–339. http://search.ebscohost.com/login.aspx?direct=true&AuthType=cookie,ip,shib,uid&db=buh&AN=5953194&site=ehost-live&scope=site

Sproat, P. A. (2007). An evaluation of the UK's anti-money laundering and asset recovery regime. *Crime, Law and Social Change, 47*(3), 169–184.

Stessens, G. (2000). *Money laundering: A new international law enforcement model.* Cambridge: Cambridge University Press.

Stigler, G. J. (1971). The theory of economic regulation. *The Bell Journal of Economics and Management Science, 2*(1), 3–21.doi:10.2307/3003160

Strauss, A., & Corbin, J. (1990). *Basics of qualitative research: Grounded theory procedures and techniques.* Newbury Park, CA, London: Sage.

Suddaby, R. (2006). From the editors: What grounded theory is not. *Academy of Management Journal, 49*(4), 633–642.

Sutinen, J. G., & Kuperan, K. (1999). A socio-economic theory of regulatory compliance. *International Journal of Social Economics, 26*(1/2/3), 174–193.

Takats, E. (2011). A theory of 'crying wolf': The economics of money laundering enforcement. *Journal of Law, Economics & Organization, 27*(1), 32–78.

Tanzi, V. (1996). *Money laundering and the international financial system.* Washington, DC.

TEDSalon. (2010). Rory Sutherland: Sweat the small stuff. London.

TEDxStanford. (2012). Baba Shiv: Sometimes it's good to give up the driver's seat. Stanford.

Treasury, H. M. (2007). The Money Laundering Regulation 2007. UK: The Stationery Office.

Trevino, L. K. (1986). Ethical decision making in organizations: A person-situation interactionist model. *The Academy of Management Review, 11*(3), 601–617. doi:10.2307/258313

Truman, D. B. (1971). *The governmental process* (Vol. 535). Knopf New York.

Turner, J. L., Mock, T. J., & Srivastava, R. P. (2002). *An analysis of the fraud triangle.* Memphis.

Tyler, T. R. (2006). *Why people obey the law.* Princeton: Princeton University Press.

Ünay, S. (2011). The rise of the regulatory state in Europe. *TJP*, 21.

Unger, B. (2013a). The history of money laundering. In B. Unger & D. van der Linde (Eds.), *Research handbook on money laundering* (pp. 19–34). Cheltenham: Edward Elgar Publishing.

Unger, B. (2013b). Introduction. In B. Unger & D. van der Linde (Eds.), *Research handbook on money laundering* (pp. 3–18). Cheltenham: Edward Elgar Publishing.

Unger, B., & Busuioc, E. M. (2007). *The scale and impacts of money laundering.* Cheltenham: Edward Elgar.

Unger, B., & van der Linde, D. (2013). *Research handbook on money laundering.* Cheltenham: Edward Elgar Publishing, Incorporated.

United Nations. (2000). *United nations convention against transnational organised crime.* New York: United Nations. https://www.unodc.org/unodc/en/treaties/CTOC/.

United Nations. (2004). *United nations convention against corruption* New York: United Nations. https://www.unodc.org/unodc/en/treaties/CAC/.

UNODC. (2013a). GPML Mandate. http://www.unodc.org/documents/money-laundering/GPML-Mandate.pdf

UNODC. (2013b). International Money-Laundering Information Network (IMoLIN)/Anti-Money-Laundering International Database (AMLID). http://www.unodc.org/unodc/en/money-laundering/imolin-amlid.html?ref=menuside

UNODC. (2013c). *UN instruments and other relevant international standards on money-laundering and terrorist financing.* http://www.unodc.org/unodc/en/money-laundering/Instruments-Standards.html?ref=menuside

Urquhart, C. (2001). An encounter with grounded theory: Tackling the practical and philosophical Issues. In E. Trauth (Ed.), *Qualitative research in IS : Issues and trends* (pp. 104–140). Hershey: Hershey, Idea Group Publising.

Urquhart, C. (2013). *Grounded theory for qualitative research: A practical guide.* Los Angeles, CA, London: SAGE.

van den Broek, M. (2011). The EU's preventive AML/CFT policy: Asymmetrical harmonisation. *Journal of Money Laundering Control, 14*(2), 170–182.

Walker, J., & Unger, B. (2009). Measuring global money laundering: 'The walker gravity model'. *Review of Law & Economics, 5*(2), 1418–1418.

Walsham, G. (1995). Interpretive case studies in IS research: Nature and method. *European Journal of Information Systems, 4*(2), 74–81.

Webb, L. (2004). A survey of money laundering reporting officers and their attitudes towards money laundering regulations. *Journal of Money Laundering Control, 7*(4), 367–375.

Weber, M., Roth, G., & Wittich, C. (1978). *Economy and society: An outline of interpretive sociology*. Berkeley: University of California Press.

Williams, C. A. (1966). Attitudes toward speculative risks as an indicator of attitudes toward pure risks. *The Journal of Risk and Insurance, 33*(4), 577–586. doi:10.2307/251231

Wolfsberg Group. (2012). *Wolfsberg anti-money laundering principles for private banking*. Geneva: The Wolfsberg Group.

Wolfsberg Group. (2014). Global banks: Global standards. http://www.wolfsberg-principles.com/index.html

Woods, M. (2012). Why bankers are more scared of New York than London. *Financial Times*. August 23, 2012. http://www.ft.com/home/uk

Wright, P., & Mukherji, A. (1999). Inside the firm: Socioeconomic versus agency perspectives on firm competitiveness. *The Journal of Socio-Economics, 28*(3), 295–307. doi:http://dx.doi.org/10.1016/S1053-5357(99)00019-0

Yan, L., Ai, L., & Tang, J. (2011). Risk-based AML regulation on internet payment services in China. *Journal of Money Laundering Control, 14*(1), 93–101.

Index

A.U. Bello, *Improving Anti-Money Laundering Compliance,* Palgrave Studies in Risk, Crime and Society,
DOI 10.1007/978-3-319-43264-9

B

C

F

G

H

I

O

P